Beyond
Shelters

Solutions to Homelessness
in Canada from the Front Lines

Beyond Shelters

Solutions to Homelessness
in Canada from the Front Lines

Edited by James Hughes

James Lorimer & Company Ltd., Publishers
Toronto

To my remarkable children Nicholas, Jenna and Frances.
Thank you for your love and the pure joy you've brought to my life.

James Lorimer & Company Ltd., Publishers acknowledges funding support from the Ontario Arts Council (OAC), an agency of the Government of Ontario. We acknowledge the support of the Canada Council for the Arts, which last year invested $153 million to bring the arts to Canadians throughout the country. This project has been made possible in part by the Government of Canada and with the support of the Ontario Media Development Corporation.

Cover design: Tyler Cleroux
Cover image: Old Brewery Mission/Monique Dykstra

Photo Credits: Rochelle Berenyi: p. 157; Pine Street Inn/Rick Friedman: p. 30 and 37; Old Brewery Mission/Monique Dykstra: p. 93 and 98; Mustard Seed/Joshua Huot: p. 170 and 172; James West of James West Photography: p. 64; Here and Now: p. 133; Heather Davis: p. 60; Edmonton Centre of Hope/Doug Schultz: p. 178; Dion Oxford: p. 118 and 122; Darius Maze: p. 218 and 220; Centre Le Havre: p. 109; Arlene Hache: p. 200

Library and Archives Canada Cataloguing in Publication

 Beyond shelters : solutions to homelessness in Canada from the front lines / edited by James Hughes.

Includes index.
Issued in print and electronic formats.
ISBN 978-1-4594-1355-9 (softcover).--ISBN 978-1-4594-1356-6 (EPUB)

 1. Shelters for the homeless--Canada. 2. Homeless persons--Canada. 3. Homelessness--Canada. I. Hughes, James, 1965-, editor

HV4509.B49 2018 362.5'92830971 C2018-904031-9
                   C2018-904032-7

James Lorimer & Company Ltd., Publishers
117 Peter Street, Suite 304
Toronto, ON, Canada
M5V 0M3
www.lorimer.ca

Printed and bound in Canada.

Contents

INTRODUCTION
The Shelterscape in Canada
James Hughes

Objectives for this volume

Over the last fifteen years, I've worked in and around the homeless sector, including reading and writing widely about the problem. There is a great deal of literature about homelessness — the size and characteristics of the homeless population, its structural origins, its regional characteristics — and the people who struggle with it — specific plights of individuals, their medical and social conditions, common paths into and out of homelessness. The diverse and numerous policy options designed to confront homelessness have also received wide coverage. However, the evolving role of homeless shelters has not received the attention it deserves. Shelters are not often enough factored into the reflections of those watching the trends and developments in the sector or designing solutions to reduce or eliminate homelessness.

To the extent they are factored in, they are too regularly stereotyped as monolithic anachronisms of an age gone by or not progressive or innovative enough to contribute to deep change. The reality could not be further from the truth.

Beyond Shelters is designed to shine a spotlight on homeless shelters and their collective power for good. Shelters have been given neither the attention nor the credit they deserve for attending to and supporting Canada's most vulnerable people usually on shoestring budgets. This collection aims to help correct this unfortunate disregard.

This book also aims to dispel the perception that shelters are all the same, serve the same people, perform the same functions and have the same vision of the future. They don't. As the chapters ahead reveal, shelters across Canada serve a wide variety of Canadians, carry out their work in very different ways and view their futures very differently. This collection brings hue and colour to the homeless shelter sector and hopefully banishes the idea that they are homogenous "one size fits all" institutions.

Beyond Shelters hopes to crack another stereotype, namely that shelters anchor the "homelessness industry," thereby serving to perpetuate homelessness. While there was some truth to this oft-cited accusation in the past, it does not reflect the reality of today's homeless shelter.

At their inception, many shelters elected to dispense only basic services such as meals, showers, beds and security — simply to help men, women and children get through the night. Clients at such shelters were asked to leave the facility during the day but invited to return again in the evening if they still had no place to go. This strictly "charitable" model of care did not take into account the very reasons that brought many guests to the shelter in the first place, namely loss of housing, health, money, support or a combination thereof. While many shelter users were able to address these challenges alone and thus navigate their way out of homelessness, many were not and found themselves needing shelter services on a continuous and sometimes permanent basis. Thus many shelters, by incorrectly assuming and in some cases expecting that all clients were well and able enough to find an exit door from homelessness without further assistance, inadvertently contributed to creating and perpetuating a chronic form of homelessness.

But they were far from alone in their lack of understanding of this vicious cycle and frankly bear little responsibility for the rise in homelessness, including in its chronic form, over the last twenty-five or so years. The lion's share of responsibility lies with governments, both federal and provincial, for numerous reasons, including cutting housing and social services to the bone in the austerity-laden 90s.[1]

Over this time, many if not most shelters have made profound changes to their missions, operations and methods. They have, to a large degree and with few exceptions, become full partners in their clients' journeys to a better place and not just a well-meaning witness to their struggle. In the chapters ahead, the authors articulate many of these stories of change and adaptation.

Beyond Shelters also explores the future of homeless sheltering in Canada. More accurately, it explores the many possible futures for these institutions, rooted as they are in community, imagination and history. The present shelter landscape can be characterized by heterogeneity, and the future promises to continue that trend. *Beyond Shelters* is about exploring the potential for those diverse futures, including the multitude of ways they can be improved. Like all our caring institutions, Canada's homeless shelters can and must do better for the complex and often desperate clientele they serve. Shelters in general have upped their game over the past two decades but remain imperfect in many ways. The authors of this collection describe many of the possible pathways forward to equip homeless shelters to more effectively contribute to ending all forms of homelessness in Canada.

Readers of this anthology will be beamed into the middle of ongoing shelter operations and there meet many homeless people whose lives have been touched by shelter staff and services. Their stories are the ones that have generated the profound and passionate desire by the shelter community for reform not only of its own practices but those of the State that serve to perpetuate the flow of homeless people to shelters' doors.

Finally, *Beyond Shelters* will introduce readers to some of the leaders in Canada's shelter community and learn about how they found their way to the service of homeless people. The collection offers a platform for these mostly current or former Directors of homeless shelters to write about the shelterscape as they know it and the ways they would propose to reform it. I have personally known many of the authors for a long time through my own work in the sector, while some I have only come to know through writing this volume. I can say with great confidence that these are all remarkable people doing remarkable work. In every corner of the country, they are quietly addressing perhaps the most complex social challenge Canada faces. They do so with great insight, humanity and humility. In addition to learning about Canadian shelters in action and the homeless people they serve, readers are about to meet a dozen or so Canadian heroes.

Shelter origins

Homeless shelters have been around for a long time. The

shelter I ran for many years, Montreal's Old Brewery Mission, was founded in 1889 — almost 130 years ago! Typical of the earliest Canadian homeless shelters, the Old Brewery had the dual function of caring for Montreal's destitute and converting them to Christianity. Old Brewery President John Wesley Palmer summarized this mission in 1905:

> *Miserable men have been helped and comforted, some who died have been decently buried and some deep in sin have been converted from their lives of sin and degradation, and changed into good and respectable citizens.*[2]

The Salvation Army preceded the Old Brewery by a few years when it opened its first "rescue homes and shelters" in 1886.[3] The Army was (and continues to be) "an international Christian church. Its message is based on the Bible; its ministry is motivated by love for God and the needs of humanity."[4]

The Social Gospel movement, which gained traction in the late nineteenth century and early twentieth century, encouraged Christians to get into communities and onto the streets to save lives and souls. This movement played a key role in how the homeless "Missions" functioned in the decades leading up to the Great Depression. The purpose of the Missions was twofold: 1) protect (usually but not exclusively) men in urban centres from hunger and exposure, and 2) save their souls for God.

Mission functions included hot meals, hot showers, clean beds . . . and church services — the latter often a compulsory condition to access the former. Today, while Toronto's Fred Victor "Mission" has become the Fred Victor "Centre" and the Old Brewery Mission has taken down the cross from its Webster Pavilion on Clark Street in Montreal, many organizations continue to have spiritual functions that echo their history of service to homeless men and women.

Shelters through the years

For a full decade leading up to the start of World War II, the Depression caused widespread misery across Canada, which became the driving force in creating the Canadian "Welfare State." With unemployment rates reaching a quarter of the adult population, views about the causes of homelessness began to change. It was seen less and less as a fault of character — as it had been over the Social Gospel period — and more a matter of circumstances. The Missions' role expanded to accommodate this growth in need, and the seeds were sown for women-specific and family shelters.

The war had a huge impact on unemployment and homelessness, largely drying up both. The federal government established "Emergency Shelter Administrators" to monitor overcrowding in cities and set up temporary housing facilities where necessary.

Homelessness and homeless sheltering remained limited and uncontroversial from the end of the war into the 1980s due to the development and reinforcement of the modern Welfare State by federal and provincial governments. Funding for housing through the *National Housing Act* in the late 1940s, mortgage guarantees by the Canadian Mortgage and Housing Corporation in the 1950s and publicly funded health care and old age security in the 1960s combined to prevent homelessness from becoming a major public issue. Through this post-war period, homeless shelters remained modestly sized and accommodated mostly middle-aged men with alcohol challenges.[5]

All this changed beginning in the 1980s with cuts to the social safety net.

The numbers

The homeless population in Canada did not simply increase over the past twenty-five years, it swelled. The Old Brewery Mission went from 150 beds in the early 1990s to more than 450 by 2015. And it is far from the largest shelter in the country. The Calgary Drop-In manages over 1,000 beds and Seaton House in Toronto, over 700.

The rise in homelessness in Canada, as in other countries, largely resulted from the federal and provincial government austerity programs that shredded the country's social safety net, not only for those at risk of homelessness but all other classes of vulnerable people as well. Elimination of the Canadian Affordable Housing program, cuts to social services by the provinces, including reductions in welfare payments and the de-institutionalization of mental health facilities all occurred within a ten-year period of one another (mid-1980s to mid-1990s) and left countless thousands of Canadians with no place to turn but the streets or shelters. Imposition of rent controls and destruction of cheap rooming houses further reduced the supply of inexpensive housing that had formerly accommodated those on the margins.

These forces have changed the face of homelessness in Canada. Homeless people are younger on average than ever before. As well, there are many more women and people from immigrant communities among the homeless population than Canada had seen in the past.

According to the most recent research (2016), there are approximately 235,000 Canadians who experience homelessness of some kind every year, and approximately 35,000 are homeless on any given night.[6] While the majority of homeless people are men, women comprise 27.3 per cent; youth represent 18.7 per cent of this population.

Federal and provincial governments have not been blind to the alarming changes in homelessness statistics. Under the leadership of then Liberal Minister of Labour, Claudette Bradshaw, the government introduced a novel anti-homelessness program in 2001 called *Supporting Communities Partnership Initiative* (nicknamed "Skippy"). The program supported shelters and other community agencies in their fight against homelessness at the local level. The program's name and priorities have changed somewhat over the years as the Liberals gave way to the Conservatives and then back again, but the program remains firmly in place. The Trudeau government has taken perhaps the most muscular approach in recent years to fighting homelessness, planning bold new investments in social and affordable housing that may disproportionately help homeless people. It remains to be seen whether these measures to repair the social safety net, when combined with new thinking and programming on the ground by shelters and other organizations serving homeless people, can heal the self-inflicted scourge of homelessness.

The shelters

Canada's homeless shelters do not manage or support all homeless people. Many people who have no permanent address try to stay with acquaintances, family or friends, and some sleep "rough" under bridges, in subway stations or abandoned buildings. The most visible homeless population, however, uses the shelters.

In 2016, Canada had slightly over four hundred "emergency" homeless shelters serving over 135,000 people.[7] Of this number, 36 per cent represent organizations serving both men and women, 29 per cent serving only men, 14 per cent strictly women, 11 per cent families and 10 per cent youth.

These shelters collectively manage almost 16,000 beds. A large majority of these beds (81 per cent) are located in urban centres and, though smaller municipalities have fewer shelter beds, they still account for nearly half (41 per cent) of all emergency shelters. Shelters in urban centres manage on average 53 beds, while shelters in smaller cities manage an average of 18 beds.[8]

The best news in the most recent research on shelter use is that, for the first time since the early 1990s, the numbers are shrinking. There have been two National Shelter Studies carried out by the Canadian Observatory on Homelessness over the past ten years, and they have shown a reduction in the shelter population by almost 20,000 people between 2005 and 2014.[9] However, the 2016 National Shelter Study also found that while the period of time most homeless people stay in a shelter is quite short (ten days), the overall average length of time actually increased between 2005 and 2014. Shelter occupancy rates have therefore increased over this time-period from 82 per cent to 92 per cent. Longer stays and higher occupancy rates reflect, among other things, a tightening of the housing market.[10]

Shelter types

To address the tremendous diversity in clientele, shelters themselves have adapted or been created to address client specificity. Shelters vary greatly in terms of size, clientele and programming. Large multi-service shelters in urban centres run on multi-million dollar budgets with hundreds of staff working 24/7 with homeless people who manifest a wide range of needs. Shelters designed to harbour women who are fleeing violence, youth shelters, Indigenous shelters and family shelters all tend to operate smaller organizations that are quite focused on their very specific clientele.

Some shelters are called "low barrier" or "no barrier" shelters, meaning the people seeking their services will not be turned away if they are inebriated or intoxicated. Such shelters often have special facilities and protocols to manage clients in such states. This approach to client admission fits within what the sector calls a "harm reduction" model. As the name suggests, this approach emphasizes reducing a homeless person's risk of suffering harm (or further harm), whether by their own hand or another's. The opposite of the harm reduction shelter is the abstinence shelter, which will not admit people who are at all under the influence of drugs or alcohol.

The Old Brewery Mission practised a policy of admitting anyone whom staff believed would not be dangerous either to clients or staff ("la politique de la dangerosité"). Shelters sometimes employ large numbers of people and have a legal obligation in all provinces and territories to offer a safe and secure workplace to their staff. This legal requirement shaped the Old Brewery's admission policies, including refusing entry to clients who did not respect the rules, for example, prohibitions on weapons or animals.

The term "emergency shelter" is the best-known descriptor for organizations that provide basic humanitarian services to homeless people — most notably food, a safe and hygienic place to sleep, showers and clothing when necessary. Over the last twenty-five years, emergency shelters have gone further and developed programs to help their clients transition out of homelessness. Many have become actual housing organizations that offer permanent or transitional housing to their formerly homeless clients.

Very few shelters in Canada today exclusively offer

emergency services. Most now offer a wide range of programs, including transitional housing, permanent housing, counseling, home search, job skills, work internships and more. I call this model "multi-functional shelters." *Beyond Shelters* concerns itself with this new model — a shelter sector that has moved beyond emergency care and become as diverse and heterogeneous as its clientele.

Housing First

Readers will hear a great deal about "Housing First" in this collection. The U.S. National Alliance to End Homelessness defines it in this way:

> *Housing First is a homeless assistance approach that prioritizes providing permanent housing to people experiencing homelessness, thus ending their homelessness and serving as a platform from which they can pursue personal goals and improve their quality of life.*[11]

From my perspective, Housing First is two things at once. It is a humane vision for the role of institutions, like shelters, that emphasizes getting homeless people into housing regardless of their condition or challenges they may face; it implies and suggests that housing is right, and homelessness is wrong. It also represents a methodology for how to rapidly and in most cases successfully, assist homeless people into homes. Many authors in *Beyond Shelters* will speak to Housing First and how its emergence over the last decade or so has affected and influenced their work.

The authors

I'm sincerely pleased to introduce readers to the authors of

Beyond Shelters. In the chapters that follow, shelter leaders from across the country (working east to west) speak to their challenges, the homeless people they serve, the way they serve them and their hopes and aspirations for how they may serve and support them in the future. They have been invited to write about their own work in or with homeless shelters as a preamble to what more shelters should be doing to reduce and eliminate homelessness in Canada. The title, *Beyond Shelters*, attempts to capture the idea that shelters can make a significant difference to the problem going forward.

The collection is led off by the father of the Housing First model (Dr. Sam Tsemberis), who describes the genesis of his work and how the approach can be deployed by homeless shelters to radically reduce homelessness in the communities they serve.

Writers from the Atlantic provinces, more specifically Fredericton (Brian Duplessis) and Corner Brook (Heather Davis), characterize and explain their local shelter work framed within political and provincial contexts that will resonate across the country. Quebec is well represented in *Beyond Shelters* by the current President and CEO of Montreal's Old Brewery Mission (Matthew Pearce). His vision of the shelter as an agent of "social reintegration" is complemented by that of the recently retired Executive Director of a small shelter in Trois-Rivières (Michel Simard) who has greatly influenced shelter work and policy development in the province. The retired CEO of the Gateway Shelter in Toronto (Dion Oxford), an individual of great patience and humanity, introduces readers to his concept of the shelter's core purpose, namely re-developing human relationships.

Moving westward, the Prairie provinces are blessed to have inspired thinkers and leaders in the shelter movement. In Winnipeg, our authors (Denisa Gavan-Koop, Tammy

Christensen and Kelly Holmes) team up to describe their upstream work with youth; in Regina, the Executive Director of Carmichael Outreach Inc. (Cora Gajari) outlines how she and her colleagues attempt to address a broad range of needs including those resulting from the trauma of colonialism and residential school system.

In Alberta, shelter leaders in Calgary (Dr. John Rook) and Edmonton (Karen Hoeft) imagine better ways of reducing and eliminating homelessness for adults.

The last two chapters offer an insightful examination of the concept of "crisis." Arlene Haché from Yellowknife pens a brave essay on "Decolonizing the North" and Trudi Shymka from The Bloom Group in Vancouver discusses the relationship between addressing homelessness and address-ing crisis.

It has been a sincere joy and a profound honour to work with each of the writers on bringing forth in clear and acces-sible ways their stories, insights, messages and hopes for the future of homeless sheltering in Canada. I'd like to thank them all for enduring the editing process, meeting deadlines and most of all for courageously sharing their narratives. These will hopefully influence the manner in which shelters change and improve in the years and decades to speed the reduction of homelessness in our country.

CHAPTER 1
Shelters and Housing First

Dr. Sam Tsemberis, International

This chapter examines the impact of Housing First on communities that introduce the model to their shelter programming. Housing First is a permanent supported housing program that is especially effective in housing that portion of the homeless population (approximately 20 per cent) characterized as "chronically homeless," "difficult to treat" and "not housing ready" by traditional homeless service providers. This cohort of individuals has complex clinical needs, utilizes disproportionately high rates of acute care services and tends toward long stays in emergency shelters. Today, there is well-documented research reporting that Housing First programs effectively engage and stably house most of this cohort.

Implementing Housing First challenges emergency homeless services to find ways to integrate shelters and other emergency programs into a system of care that provides immediate access to permanent housing for frequent shelter users. In this chapter, I explore the question of what happens to shelters and other acute care and transitional services when Housing First is introduced. To answer this question we interviewed three Housing First proponents. In this article, research evidence is presented from three perspectives: 1) individuals with long histories of homelessness and shelter use, 2) program directors of agencies operating shelters and 3) policy-makers and Housing First advocates. I also discuss the challenges faced by each constituency and describe how Housing First addressed them.

What happens when a shelter user is introduced to Housing First?

Clifford's (not his real name) experience of homelessness in New York City included over twenty years of being on and off the streets, frequenting meal programs, drop-in centres, riding the E train (and only the E train), and staying in too-many-to-name church and municipal shelters. His journey illustrates the usefulness and limitations of the City's shelter and emergency services approach for individuals who are homeless and have complex problems. As I said before, Clifford represents about 20 per cent of the homeless population that is characterized as "chronically homeless" and "high users" of acute care services (Aubry et al., 2013; Poulin, Maguire, Metraux & Culhane, 2011).

Communities sometimes struggle to discern whether a client belongs to the 20 per cent needing a Housing First intervention or falls into the 80 per cent that can be adequately served by temporary shelter support. The acute 20 per cent tend to be identified by multiple return visits to shelters — or the streets or emergency rooms or jail.

Clifford

I was both surprised and intrigued when Clifford began his reply to my interview question by talking about how he was extremely shy as a teenager (Clifford, May 12, 2018):

> *Well, it all started because I was terribly shy and anxious, especially around girls. That was all through the first years of high school, and then one summer my mother sent me to stay with my aunt in South Carolina. That's when I discovered alcohol. Right from the start, when I had a drink, my problems were gone. I was Mr. Big from NY! The girls flocked around me. I could even go to a disco and dance. I could do things I could never do before.*

Clifford reached his insight into the origins of his problems with alcohol and drugs following years of hard work on his self-care and self-help, Alcoholics Anonymous meetings and treatment. He continued . . .

> *Drinking became a way of life. Soon after high school I got a job on Wall Street, with a decent salary and that's when the drinking really took off. Everybody I worked with was also drinking, so it didn't seem like a problem. After work a bunch of us went to McCann's Bar. I had saved some money and one day about seven years later, after getting my paycheck and drinking it all up, I never went back to work. It was not long after that that I couldn't pay my rent and was evicted and ended up on the streets. My parents were ashamed of me. My mother warned me that if she saw me on TV at*

Christmas during one of those "feed the homeless"
stories she would never speak to me again.

For Clifford, the trajectory into homelessness was less like falling off a ledge than down a long flight of stairs. At each step down, family, friends and other supports become either exhausted or frustrated. With each successive loss he was one step closer to the street. In Clifford's case, his parents helped, then stopped; his brother helped for a while but at some point, Clifford understood he could not continue to stay on his brother's couch and disrupt his life. For Clifford, taking the final step meant wandering the streets, drinking by day and riding the E train at night.

He continues . . .

That's when I started using shelters. I had to get
cleaned up and had to eat. The first place I went to
was part of John Heuss House, a drop-in program
around Wall Street. At night, buses would come
and take some of us to a church and then wake us
at 5 a.m. to bring us back. When I missed the bus,
I stayed out on the street and if it was too cold, I
would go to the Ferry Terminal.

There are networks of small shelters operated by non-profits or religious organizations that provide immediate short-term help. Some regular drop-in centre clients utilize these nightly shelters for years. They are a useful alternative to large municipal shelters. Clifford preferred the small church shelters. Makeshift spaces consisting of eight to fifteen cots set up each evening in either the narthex or basement of the church. Meals were served by volunteers who infused the evening with an element of kindness. The beds are few, and demand for them is high. It is first come, first served, and the more organized and sober clients were better able to secure beds for the night.

The default shelters were the large municipal shelters; Clifford visited several of these on and off for years. He describes his experience this way:

> *They were scary places. The staff spoke like they were giving commands: "show your ID," "get in line," "you have to be on time to get breakfast." You could not come in before a certain hour, and you could not leave before a certain hour. You could be drinking but had to look like you were not drunk. You had to keep appointments with counsellors or else you could not stay there. Some of these shelters had working people staying in them. I thought to myself, "if I could be that organized and keep all those appointments, I would not be homeless." I could not meet the curfews or make all the meetings. Meal times were too strict, and I missed many meals and safety was always an issue. There were lots of different client groups running things or selling you things. Sometimes, the people with TV cameras would show up, and that's when I would go and hide. It was hard finding a place to hide or even a private space to change my clothes. But I could not stop drinking so that's where I was. I would drink, get sick and start all over again. Sometimes I would wake up in Bellevue [Psychiatric Hospital] and had no idea how I got there or why I was there. They wanted to keep me or send me to the state psychiatric hospital, and all I wanted to do was get out. The staff would bargain*

with me: "stay for another week voluntarily, and
we won't take you to court."

Sitting across the table and listening to this sixty-year-old, articulate, slightly stocky, African American man with an infectious smile, it was sometimes difficult to reconcile the discrepancy between the man he was describing in his story and the person sitting in front of me today.

> *I got to know where I could stay, where to eat,*
> *and got to know a lot of people in my situation.*
> *One day I heard about a new soup kitchen on*
> *East 109th Street and Central Park. I walked in*
> *and was met at the door by Rory Gilbert. After*
> *a few meals Rory asked me if he could introduce*
> *me to another program, a housing program, and*
> *I agreed. A day later, he brings me over and*
> *this guy comes over to me and says, "Hi I'm Ben*
> *Tallerson, welcome to Pathways to Housing!"*
> *[Ben was the peer-specialist assistant team leader*
> *of the East Harlem Pathways Housing First*
> *team.] When I explained to Ben that I was*
> *homeless and drinking a lot and getting sick a lot*
> *he said, "That's because you are drinking lousy*
> *beer. You should drink Budweiser."*

This was not a reception Clifford had experienced previously. Ben welcomed him warmly, put him at ease and joked a bit about the drinking problems that, in the absence of Housing First, had made him vulnerable to a quick eviction. He felt understood and accepted, not judged or expected to change to be admitted. Clifford agreed on that first day to work with the program. Three weeks later he moved into an apartment of his own. For several months after moving in, he stored the clothes he wore that day under his pillow. A few years later, he began to work again but still struggled with his drinking and his weight.

"How has getting a place of your own changed your life?" I ask.

> *Well, I used to be afraid that my family would see me on TV during one of those "help the homeless on the holidays" stories. I think about that all the time when the TV shows people waiting in line in soup kitchens or lining up for shelter beds. Only now, I am sitting in my living room and watching this on my TV.*

In numerous studies and randomized clinical trials involving thousands of people, more than 80 per cent of individuals like Clifford have demonstrated that with the proper long-term rent subsidy and support services most can be successfully housed without having first achieved sobriety or freedom from psychiatric symptoms.

Housing acquisition can often come quickly, and housing stability is achieved by a willingness of the program to rehouse clients as needed. Over time, there is often an improvement regarding clinical conditions and quality of life. Once housed, people like Clifford receive substantial support by service teams that provide regular home visits. One can make the case that by implementing Housing First we can end homelessness for most of the acute 20 per cent. The challenge is that most communities operate only a small number of Housing First programs. How can communities move beyond modest individual successes and bring Housing First to scale?

What Is Housing First?

As Housing First becomes widely disseminated, variations in way the program is defined have emerged. Notably, governments in the U.S. and Canada have attempted to implement a cheap version of Housing First, sometimes called rapid-rehousing, providing only brief rent subsidies and minimally staffed and trained support services while nonetheless continuing to expect full-fledged successful results. Instead, at least half the clients experience a revolving door of evictions.

Housing First refers to the Pathways Housing First program (Tsemberis, 2015). This is a well-documented, complex clinical intervention based on a consumer-directed philosophy that includes independent housing with permanent rental subsidies and support services adequate to meet client needs as two key program components. This model has produced positive research outcomes and is being disseminated throughout Canada, the U.S., European Union and New Zealand (Padgett, Henwood & Tsemberis, 2016).

Clifford, with a persistent substance abuse problem and mental health problems, is exactly the type of person that Housing First was designed to serve. The program breaks from age-old homeless services that require sobriety, psychiatric treatment and program compliance as preconditions for shelter. This traditional model may make sense for some shelter residents who are able to manage these regimens. Housing First allows for the most vulnerable 20 per cent of shelter residents, who have proven unable to comply with such preconditions, to obtain permanent housing and supports.

Housing First turns the predominant treatment-compliance-then-housing system on its head by offering people like Clifford immediate access to an apartment of his own with no time limits and with supports in place. Its bold refusal to require sobriety, abstinence, psychiatric treatment compliance or compliance with curfews or program rules as preconditions for receiving housing represents a paradigm shift. Rather than housing being offered as reward for treatment compliance or good behaviour, it is offered as a basic human right.

Under the Housing First model, apartments are rented from community landlords. The program pays a rent subsidy, and participants pay 30 per cent of their income (if they have any). Participants live in "normal" housing that is socially integrated into the community. They are expected to meet the terms and conditions of a standard lease and must also agree to accept a regular home visit by a member of the support services team (Tsemberis, 2015).

It is important to distinguish Housing First from other traditional programs where housing and services are both located in the same building (a single-site program). Exits or evictions from single-site programs result in the loss of housing as well as discontinuation of support services. In Housing First programs, services are in the community but remain separate from the housing. If clients are evicted from their apartments by the landlord, they are not discharged from the support services. In fact, support service staff will help them through the crisis of eviction and assist with moving them into another unit.

Support services staff consists of some combination of social workers, mental health counselors, addiction specialists, peer specialists and can include nurses and other treatment professionals. Staff all make regular home visits to support the well-being of the client. The program uses a harm reduction approach and a stages-of-change theoretical framework, trauma-informed care and other clinical interventions with proven effectiveness for the conditions faced by this population (Prochaska & DiClemente, 1983).

This consumer-directed approach is the philosophical foundation of the entire program. Participants with complex problems are welcomed, accepted and encouraged to set their own goals. Client choice drives the type and sequence of services. Since most clients want housing as the very first step, the program became known as "Housing First" — it was the first service that most clients requested when given a real choice.

The consumer-directed service and treatment approach of Housing First is consistent with the principles and practices of recovery-focused care (Anthony, 2000). The treatment and support offered after a person is housed contributes to achieving high rates of housing stability and improvements in self-reported quality of life. Housing First programs have consistently achieved an 80 per cent rate of housing stability compared to 40 per cent of treatment-first approaches, which lack the commitment to rehouse (Aubry et al., 2015).

What happens when a shelter program adopts a Housing First approach?

The recent changes in Canada's Homelessness Partnering Strategy (2014) requires communities and programs to change practice and funding allocations for their homeless programs. The Strategy requires communities to allocate approximately 50 per cent of their federal funds to programs that emphasize ending chronic homelessness by implementing Housing First programs. For example, programs that operate transitional housing programs aimed at improving individuals' clinical conditions to get them "housing ready" need to change their mandate and operation; this is based on research that found such programs to be less effective in getting people housed than programs that provided Housing First and then worked on addressing clinical problems (Aubry et. al., 2015).

Although similar policies exist in the U.S., the policy has not been supported by an allocation of funding or other resources and therefore overall systems change has stalled. There is considerable variation among EU nations with regard to implementing Housing First, with several member nations adopting Housing First as national policy and funding it to achieve scale.

In each community and country, local champions of Housing First have emerged. Many agencies in the U.S. that provide shelter and transitional housing were so impressed by evidence of Housing First's effectiveness that they took it upon themselves to transform their programs to focus on permanent housing for the most vulnerable 20 per cent. The steps taken by one of these agencies serves as a useful example to illustrate how Housing First programs can be initiated and expanded.

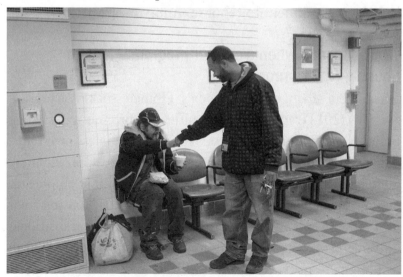

The lobby of Pine Street Inn, a Housing First shelter in Boston, Massachusetts.

Based in Boston, Massachusetts, Pine Street Inn has been operating programs to assist homeless individuals for more than four decades. It operates street outreach, drop-in centres, emergency shelters and supportive housing. Pine Street Inn is a renowned Boston homeless service provider and the subject of many stories including a memoir (made into a movie) by poet Nick Flynn.

Many years ago, when Flynn was employed by Pine Street Inn as an outreach worker, one of the people he encountered on the streets during his shift one rainy night was a middle-aged man with long, gray hair who was visibly very drunk, sitting on the sidewalk and leaning against a building wall. When Flynn approached, the man was cantankerous and swore at him to leave him alone. However, Flynn was patient and persisted; in the conversation that ensued he was shocked to learn that this man lying on the sidewalk was his long-lost father whom he had not seen since childhood (Flynn, 2004).

Lyndia Downie has been Executive Director of Pine Street Inn for thirty-five years. About ten years ago, as the evidence for Housing First was mounting, Lyndia led the staff, clients and the Board of Directors on a strategic plan to transform the agency's approach to homelessness for their long-term clients likely to benefit from Housing First.

Research in implementation science indicates that multiple factors can support or inhibit successful program dissemination. Damschroder and her colleagues (2009) list five domains: knowledge of the intervention, inner setting (host agency), outer setting (local community), individuals involved (local champions) and the process (e.g., attention paid to training, evaluation and program fidelity).

At Pine Street Inn, Downie served as a local champion and ensured that everyone in the agency was knowledgeable about the Housing First program, why it was relevant to their services and what they needed to modify in their internal systems and practices to effectively implement the Housing First model. In addition to educating the agency staff and Board about Housing First, Pine Street Inn hired a researcher to determine the average time taken by program participants to progress from admission to permanent supportive housing. Preliminary findings indicated that it had been taking an average of eight years. These evaluation results further motivated Pine Street Inn to introduce Housing First and quickly transition shelter clients to their expanding portfolio of Permanent Supported Housing (PSH) Housing First beds.

Introducing systems change

How does one redesign a system comprised of programs and practices that require multi-year treatment and a long period of sobriety as preconditions for housing to include as a key component a Housing First program that takes a person from the street to permanent housing in a matter of weeks?

In a recent interview, Downie commented,

> *We had really bought into the "housing readiness" approach . . . We really believed people had to be housing ready, and this was reinforced by our funding model because we did not have deep social services funding attached to our housing. We could only house people that did not require a lot of follow-up support [in order to not set them up for eviction or other failure in the absence of such supports].*

Once Pine Street Inn embraced the approach that shelters can be part of the solution to ending homelessness, they took two bold steps:

First, we changed our admission criteria for the shelter programs and no longer required sobriety or treatment compliance in all our shelters. This was huge for us, but we realized that if shelters would participate in a Housing First approach they had to serve the function of low barrier or barrier-free points of entry.

Pine Street Inn converted their shelter programs and emergency beds to "wet" shelters programs, meaning that clients did not have to be "dry" or sober to be admitted. The second step required a major leap of faith for Downie, the staff and the Board of Directors.

We decided to convert one of our thirty-unit transitional housing programs into Housing First — permanent, supported housing, off-site support services, using a harm reduction approach, and all the other Housing First criteria. This represented a financial risk and an enormous change in agency philosophy and practice. But we had to go back and ask ourselves, "aren't we in this to end homelessness?" We had to recommit to our core values.

The agency voluntarily requested a change in the funding they were receiving from the Massachusetts State government. Pine Street Inn asked that the funds to operate one of their thirty-bed transitional housing programs be converted to thirty rent supplements (Section 8 vouchers) and case management support services so that it could rent thirty scattered-site apartments.

> *We went all-in in adopting Housing First. We did not select the most compliant shelter residents for Housing First. Instead, we decided to select thirty of our chronic shelter users with complex needs to occupy these permanent housing slots and see what happens.*

Support services were put in place to meet the complex needs of the newly housed tenants. In all, these were enormous changes for an agency with a long history of successful programs.

> *It was a struggle to learn to operate a new program with different practices and different values, but the twelve-month follow-up data showed an 80 per cent housing retention rate for that first cohort of thirty clients.*

Identifying individuals who were chronically homeless and who kept cycling in and out of shelter systems or proved "non-compliant" or "not-housing ready" and enrolling them into a Housing First program had proven effective in another larger shelter system in Westchester County (Stefancic & Tsemberis, 2007). County officials there, concerned about the growing number of individuals who fit this profile, sought out Pathways to Housing to serve this "non-compliant" sector of homeless clients.

Editorials and letters to the editor objected to the presumed irresponsibility of giving apartments to those who were drug-addicted and mentally ill without first requiring that prospective tenants attain sobriety and stability. Interestingly, the leading organizers and representatives of this opposition came primarily from the local shelter providers and homeless services community (Felton, 2003). Not everyone was opposed; some program administrators told Felton in confidence that the Pathways approach was a "paradigm shift" (p. 316) and an improvement on the "Elizabethan" requirements (p. 317) of local programs.

In what would prove to be a common objection as dissemination of the Pathways Housing First approach gathered steam, several providers argued that they were "already doing it." Felton (2003) points out that the expected NIMBY ("not in my backyard") response by residents and community organizations did not materialize, perhaps due to the use of scattered-site apartments as opposed to a single-site building that would have attracted attention. Soon after implementation, and as more of the population identified to be served were housed, opposition eased up and Pathways settled into the community and continued to house clients no other agency wanted to serve. A year later, the Pathways contract was renewed, and the program was declared successful, with fifty-four chronically homeless men and women successfully housed.

Pine Street Inn: One year later

The following year, the Pine Street Inn requested more vouchers from the State in lieu of transitional housing funds; it then proceeded to slowly and consistently increase its supply of permanent supportive housing each year after that.

> *As we increased the number of permanent housing beds, what we realized is that by the third year we had empty shelter beds — in the winter! At that point, we requested the State to close one of our small thirty-five-bed shelters and used the funds for Housing First.*

Shelter beds at Pine Street Inn were reduced in tandem with a significant increase in PSH use of a Housing First approach; it did not involve a hasty dismantling of the shelters as safety net programs.

On a policy level there is another lesson to be learned from the collaboration between the Pine Street Inn and the State of Massachusetts. The agency advocated for contract changes, and the government funder was receptive and agreed to change contract goals and funding based on a collaborative, data-informed dialogue. This offers a constructive example of how contracts between the funder and the provider agency can be negotiated in collaboration, based on agency needs and client outcomes. This process can begin with shared goals between agency and funder. From there, the contract can be developed to ensure these goals are met. Such mutually negotiated contracts can be based on performance and outcomes rather than monitoring and audit functions and provide clear direction and adequate funding for who is served and how to best serve them.

Making shelters more efficient

What had not been anticipated but was readily welcomed was the improvement in shelter efficiency and capacity realized by introducing a Housing First program for long-term shelter users. Here is an oversimplified example of how long-term users can affect shelter capacity: If an agency is operating a thirty-bed shelter, seven nights a week, 365 days a year, and the long-term residents are staying in the shelter for an average of six months, then that thirty-bed shelter can only serve sixty individuals a year (thirty residents at six months each). However, if the individuals who are chronically homeless are moved into a Housing First program, and that shelter operates as an emergency shelter, in which the

average length of stay is twenty-one days, then that same
shelter can serve 521 individuals a year. The same number
of shelter beds can be more efficiently used, serve a larger
number of individuals and can begin to focus the funding
toward increasing the availability of permanent supported
housing, i.e., Housing First.

The Pine Street Inn transition is especially inspiring
because it was voluntary and self-directed. The agency
embraced the Housing First program for the right reasons
— to serve the most vulnerable with permanent housing and
supports. This was not imposed by a change in government
rules in which the agency had to comply. This was a successful agency that realized there was a more effective way to
end homelessness for this group and voluntarily took steps
to implement difficult and enormous cultural and operational changes because it was in the best interest of these
clients. It appears that this approach is often an efficient use
of taxpayer dollars as it costs less to provide Housing First
than ongoing acute and emergency care to someone who
remains homeless.

Settling in: one of Pine Street Inn's Housing First tenants.

Lessons learned

Pine Street Inn learned a great deal during this transformation. The Housing First program's housing retention rate is still approximately 83 per cent, and the agency has made great strides in providing effective support services. Downie emphasizes that the greatest operational challenges have been in providing the right amount of support services, managing the 24/7 emergency on-call system, addressing landlord concerns and helping clients to deal with loneliness and other tenants as visitors.

Downie notes that philosophically, it was a huge challenge to adopt a harm reduction approach to housing and services, "giving out housing as a matter of right, especially after all those years of using housing as a reward." However, she emphasizes that it was immediately fulfilling to operate in this new way, noting, "When we introduced Housing First and could offer clients a place of their own, it was the first time our long-stay clients could see a road out of homelessness."

On reflecting how the agency culture and practice has changed since the program's inception, she provides a quick list of other lessons learned:

> *Let people who are struggling into housing first; we have seen that those who need help the most cannot access it; it's our job to figure out how to engage and provide the right supports; don't assume you know which people won't do well; support services (relationship) is the glue.*

In the past fifteen years, the Pine Street Inn has made a modest reduction from 715 shelter beds to 670 shelter beds (representing a change from 72 per cent of the agency's total beds to 41 per cent of total beds, involving shorter lengths of stay) and has increased their housing stock from 995 units of permanent supportive housing to 1,623 units (from 28 per cent of the agency's total beds to 59 per cent). Working collaboratively with other agencies in Boston that are now also using Housing First, the number of homeless persons on the streets of Boston has decreased in each of the past three years.

What happens to shelters when Housing First becomes national policy?

A tale of homelessness in two cities

Professor Eoin O'Sullivan of Trinity University in Dublin, Ireland, offers an insightful analysis describing the impact differing national policies have on shelters, permanent housing and outcomes for people experiencing homelessness (O'Sullivan, 2017). He selected two cities and countries for this analysis: Dublin, Ireland, and Helsinki, Finland. O'Sullivan's full analysis, which will be published in a forthcoming book, also includes Denmark and Norway, but Ireland and Finland best illustrate the point (O'Sullivan, personal communication, June 20, 2018).

DUBLIN

While there are considerable differences in culture, socio-economic status and political orientation between Ireland and Finland, from the narrow perspective of homelessness, the two countries had enough in common for a meaningful comparison of their policies and the consequences of those policies.

Ireland has a population of 4.75 million, with about one-third living in Dublin. Finland has a population of 5.5 million, with about one-quarter living in Helsinki. In 2008, each country developed a ten-year plan to end rough sleeping (homelessness), but each nation adopted a very different policy approach to achieve this goal.

Soon after the plan was adopted, Ireland's economy was profoundly affected by the world-wide economic crisis. Ireland quickly invested in creating more emergency shelters and other emergency accommodation as a means of stemming the tide in the increased numbers of "rough sleepers" (individuals sleeping on the streets or other public places).

Ireland, like many Western countries, had historically increased shelter bed availability during emergencies, only to find that the shelters were still present and fully occupied long after the crisis had abated. Looking at a broader period, from 1985 to 2018, the number of shelter beds in Ireland increased from 600 to 2,100 (O'Sullivan, 2017). Emergency accommodation also included paying for motel or hotel rooms on a nightly basis.

Using this emergency response approach, the number of people who were homeless in Ireland between 2008 and 2017 increased from 1,200 to 5,400. Due to this disappointing increase in numbers of homeless people, Ireland recently adopted a Housing First approach that is focused on creating direct access to permanent supported housing, and in 2018 appointed a national Housing First director (Upshaw, 2018).

HELSINKI

In the early part of the new century, Finland adopted a Housing First approach as part of its national policy on homelessness. The policy was grounded in a belief that housing is a basic human right, and the national government was willing to commit funding to support that belief. Finland correctly understood that successfully moving a person who is homeless directly into housing would reduce the need to invest in more shelters or transitional housing.

The Y-Foundation, established in 1985, worked closely with the Government of Finland to implement the Housing First policy. This national foundation, located in Helsinki, richly endowed with funds from the government, business community and faith community, was charged with ending homelessness. The Y-Foundation and its funders committed to the Housing First philosophy: treating housing as a basic human right and utilizing a harm reduction strategy for addressing problems with addiction.

Having fully adopted the national Housing First philosophy, the Y-Foundation began to address the problem by taking several steps, including prioritizing subgroups among the homeless, converting shelters to permanent housing and developing or acquiring many buildings and apartments (Y-Foundation, 2017). In all, from 2008 to 2018, approximately 16,000 units of all types of housing were converted, developed or acquired by the foundation. Some of the 16,000 units were rented to individuals who were homeless and had complex needs, and many others were rented at market rate to any tenants in the community.

In 2008, the country passed legislation that allocated some of the profits from the national lottery to converting shelters from large warehouse-like spaces with many cots into small, 200-square-foot individual sleeping units with shared facilities. While the small, studio-like units afforded greater privacy and were more dignified than shelter cots, the process led to a significant reduction in shelter beds available as shelters converted.

The shelters could be renovated or razed and rebuilt as permanent housing quickly because they used existing land and locations and thus did not need to acquire new land, obtain community approval for siting the programs nor deal with other time-consuming legal protocols. In addition to converting shelter beds, Finland and the Y-Foundation made extraordinary investments in purchasing, renovating, developing and otherwise acquiring permanent housing.

This impressive real estate portfolio serves to create a socially and economically integrated housing model. However, Finland's Housing First approach shows some significant variations from the Pathways evidence-based Housing First model used in North America. Much of the permanent housing in Finland is single-site, whereas the Pathways programs driven by client choice are comprised of predominately scattered-site units integrated into the community. In Finland, the single-site housing acts as transitional housing, from which clients can graduate to scattered-site apartments of their own. While this process of graduation from low demand to higher demand housing is inconsistent with high-fidelity Housing First programs, it certainly offers a practical solution to political and neighbourhood pressures faced while securing community consent for these projects.

Finland's program is also somewhat compromised on the issue of consumer choice for both housing and services. Consumers are offered units that are available in a large building on a take-it-or-leave-it basis. There is no real choice about location with a single-site building. The single-site programs are carefully supervised, another practical necessity with this model that also cannot be left to consumer choice.

On the positive side of program fidelity, the single-site housing does offer low demand, permanent housing, including immediate access to housing, no treatment or sobriety required, a program commitment to rehouse and tenants need only abide by the terms and conditions of a standard lease and a home visit (Stefancic et al., 2013). Support services for tenants with complex needs are not provided by the Y-Foundation but through community social service agencies, thus keeping housing separate from services.

The Y-Foundation real estate portfolio includes many more full-market-price units than subsidized units, thus ensuring the entire real estate portfolio's financial sustainability. It is a profitable business operated by a not-for-profit agency that reinvests profits into the management, upkeep and improvement of the housing.

By adopting Housing First as the national policy and taking this approach toward reducing reliance on shelters and greatly increasing the supply of permanent and affordable housing, the number of shelter beds in Finland between 1985 and 2017 decreased from 2,100 to fifty. This was the number of shelter beds in Helsinki as of Y-Foundation reporting in 2017(Y-Foundation, 2017).

How can fifty shelter beds possibly be sufficient for a population of over a million inhabitants? This is perhaps where Finland has accomplished more than most other nations. Several years ago, Finland contributed the crowning touch to its plan to end homelessness when its legislature approved a national homelessness prevention plan, designed to identify subgroups of the population that are currently housed but deemed to be at high risk for homelessness. The identification process is based on an analysis of individual and family income relative to rent expenses. If their rent burden puts them at risk for homelessness, the individuals or families qualify for the program and are provided with a rent supplement to prevent their eviction.

Using these three combined strategies: 1) a Housing First, or what the Europeans call a "housing led" (compared to a "shelter led") approach as a matter of national policy; 2) a sustained, entrepreneurial and non-profit approach of acquiring and managing housing; and 3) active use of an effective prevention strategy, the number of beds for people experiencing homelessness in Finland has decreased to fifty.

Juha Kaakinen, Executive Director of the Y-Foundation, confirms this astonishing reality. "We have reached what the Canadians call 'functional zero.' No one is homeless here for more than ten days. With so many units under the Foundation's management there is always a unit available to house the next person."

Finland is the first member nation in Europe that has essentially ended homelessness using Housing First. Norway and many other EU nations, like Canada, have adopted and funded Housing First as a significant part of their national policy. The results in Finland are inspiring to all.

In my interview with Juha Kaakinen, he describes what seems like a practical, analytical and problem-solving approach to their work. "We saw Housing First as a way to solve the problem and as the right thing to do."

His response is reminiscent of Michael Moore's movie *Where to Invade Next* (Deal, Lessin & Moore, 2015), in which Moore talks about wanting to steal Finland's educational system and bring it to the United States (Finland's students score highest in educational achievement, while the U.S. students lag behind most Western countries). In one scene, Moore interviews a Finnish high school math teacher and asks him what he demands from his students. "I just want them to have fun in school," replies the teacher. "But you are the *math* teacher!" exclaims an exacerbated Moore in mock protest when he does not receive the punitive or competitive response he has been raised to expect.

In the same way, Finland reduced chronic homelessness because it was the right and smart thing to do. While it is accurate to say that in and of themselves the steps taken by the Finns are not new discoveries, and in fact they can be implemented by any city or nation with the political will to enact them, there are two things that Kaakinen said probably account for the uniqueness of Finland's spectacular success.

The first was consensus:

> *Once we committed to Housing First and to end chronic homelessness, we really built a consensus about the model and how to achieve it. Everyone was on board — the national government, local governments, the business community, the faith community and providers. We all worked in the same direction towards the same goal.*

And the other relates to cultural values:

> *The values of this model — housing as a right, social inclusion and a commitment to helping those who are less fortunate by asking those who are more fortunate to contribute more. As a society we are mostly aligned on these values.*

So what will it take for other cities and countries to get to the "Finnish line" on homelessness?

CHAPTER 2
Mitigating Harm to Women
Heather Davis, Corner Brook, NL

Shelter work

Unless you have needed to stay in a domestic violence shelter or you work in the area of violence against women, you likely have only the barest of knowledge about what goes on behind the locked doors of a transition house. Transition houses in Newfoundland and Labrador provide essential services for women and children escaping violence — first and foremost, a safe place to stay. Services also include transportation to the shelter, provision of basic necessities such as food and hygiene products, safety planning, supportive counseling, assistance with applications to legal aid, financial supports for public housing and advocacy for the needs of women and their families.

Unlike many of our activist sisters in the women's community, transition houses typically operate quietly, behind closed doors. Women who have lived with violence need time to process, breathe, be validated and make decisions about what happens next in their lives. Transition houses offer a safe, non-judgmental space for these regenerative moments to occur, and shelter staff offer support no matter what a woman decides to do when she leaves. The cycle of violence can often include a shelter stay. It is common for women to leave and return to abusive partners many times. Shelter staff understand this cycle and the importance of remaining a supportive constant in a woman's life regard-less of the choices she makes. In this way, shelters lessen the isolation and shame attached to the cycle a woman is caught in and offer a nurturing place where she knows she is welcome to return.

Shelter workers typically work 24/7, and their crisis intervention work includes acting as a liaison with other agencies on a woman's behalf, accompanying her to court, watching her children so she can attend appointments and listening when she needs to talk. Attending to these needs, it is the hope that when a woman departs a shelter, she is in a healthier and safer place than when she arrived.

Origins

Like elsewhere in Canada, women's shelters in Newfoundland and Labrador grew directly out of a community desire to address violence against women. Advocates for women drew attention to domestic violence as a widespread community problem. The development and redevelopment of safe spaces for women in Newfoundland and Labrador continues to be shaped by community activism.

The women's movement made formal inroads into many small communities across Canada after the establishment of the Royal Commission on the Status of Women in Canada in 1967 and the United Nation's International Women's Year in 1975. This wave of feminism took hold in some of the farthest reaches of the country, including Newfoundland and Labrador, spurring on feminist leaders to press governments and lead communities on a variety of issues, including family violence.

The establishment of transition houses in Newfoundland and Labrador, a province of approximately 500,000 people, spans a few decades. St. John's, the provincial capital and largest centre in Newfoundland and Labrador, was the first to establish a transition house in the province; Iris Kirby House opened in 1981. Located in downtown St. John's on Garrison Hill, this shelter began its work by providing four emergency shelter beds, supported by a small staff complement. In 1984, Iris Kirby House moved to Bond Street with a slight increase in shelter capacity to eight beds. Its final move was to Waterford Bridge Road in 1994. This allowed for a sizeable expansion to twenty-two shelter beds, with increased programming and a larger staff comprised of twenty permanent employees along with relief staff. This project was funded by the Rotary Club of St. John's.

In 2013, Iris Kirby House began a two-year transformation to better respond to the increasing demand for service from women and children escaping relationship violence. A capital renovation included redevelopment of the main residential structure from one to two units to increase capacity and allow for some separate living space for those women without children. The renovation also provided for four self-contained, supportive housing units adjoining the shelter. These units are available to women leaving the shelter, those who cannot stay in a communal living situation or those who require additional time and skill development to be able to move to more independent second-stage living. The St. John's shelter expansion also allowed for ten additional emergency shelter beds, bringing the number at this site to thirty-two.

The most recent women's shelter to open (2010) was, interestingly, an offshoot of Iris Kirby House. A community assessment conducted in 2006 had demonstrated increasing demand for safe shelter and programs closer to home from women in the Conception Bay Centre and Conception Bay North areas. Iris Kirby House responded to the need through redevelopment of a former convent property in Carbonear, which was gifted to it in 2009 by the Presentation Sisters. The resulting facility, "O'Shaughnessy House," opened in 2010 and includes fifteen emergency beds for women and their children escaping relationship violence. Iris Kirby House Inc. now provides supportive housing to both shelters, the self-contained apartments and nine additional second-stage apartments in various locations in the St. John's and Carbonear areas.

Status of Women Councils were involved in developing shelters in many areas. As Iris Kirby House was being planned, work also was underway in Corner Brook to set up a shelter. In 1980, the Corner Brook Status of Women Council called a public meeting to discuss the issue of family violence. Because the number of women seeking support from the Women's Centre around issues of family violence was so high, the Council established a committee to examine education, awareness and service provision. A grant was received to research the need for a refuge for women. This research found that in a ten-month period, 231 cases of "wife abuse" had been reported in Corner Brook alone, a small city of fewer than 25,000 people. During the next three years, constant lobbying of the public, businesses, community groups and all levels of government resulted in the establishment of Transition House (now known as

Willow House.) Staff were hired, and the first West Coast shelter opened in 1983.

Shelters in other parts of the province were established in a similar way, and in this regard, Newfoundland was no different than other parts of the country. The origin stories are all very similar. In Labrador City, a town in Western Labrador with a population of less than 10,000, a committee started to research the need for a shelter in 1982. By 1984, the Family Crisis Centre opened (now known as Hope Haven) and was run solely by volunteers and funded through donations from the community. The following year the Family Crisis Centre was incorporated and received a whopping $2,000 per year in funding from the provincial government.

Around the same time in Central Labrador, the idea of a shelter serving Happy Valley–Goose Bay was starting to develop. Libra House was formally established in 1985. Cara House in Gander opened in 1991 as a refuge for women and children fleeing violence. Planning work and lobbying had begun years earlier with significant involvement from the Gander Status of Women. In 1987, a committee was formed with the goal of establishing a transition house in central Newfoundland. As with other centres, it took years of determined effort to see a shelter opened. Grace Sparkes House in Marystown was planned as it became clear the number of women having to leave the Burin Peninsula to travel to St. John's more than warranted a safe shelter for women in this area of the province. Grace Sparkes House officially opened in October 2000, again following many years of lobbying by concerned citizens and service providers on the Burin Peninsula, who made it their mission to ensure the women and children in their area had a safe haven for support.

In Nunatsiavut, the Inuit land claim area for Northern Labrador Inuit people, the first women's shelter opened in Hopedale in 1995. Initially, this was a rental unit, and in 1996 a new safe house was built. That same year, Jupp Cottage opened in Nain, a community in Northern Labrador. These safe houses were run by volunteers and the local women's group. The safe houses at this time relied on local charity and fundraisers to pay the bills. According to *Safe Houses in Northern Labrador* (Wolfrey, 1998), there were no safe houses in the communities of Postville, Makkovik and Rigolet, and women were forced to stay with family, use the nursing station, or run away from their communities. It should be noted that at this time there was no police force in these communities. At present, after lobbying efforts from women in Nunatsiavut, there are three women's shelters fully funded by the Newfoundland and Labrador Government: Nain Safe House, Hopedale Women's Shelter and Kirkina House, located in Rigolet.

As shelters for abused women and their children began opening across Newfoundland and Labrador in the 1980s, it became obvious that a provincial association, which could provide essential support services to these organizations, was needed. In 1987, the Provincial Association Against Family Violence was established and is now known as the Transition House Association of Newfoundland and Labrador (THANL). Members include all provincially funded shelters in the province, both the island portion and Labrador. THANL serves to strengthen the network of shelters (including transition houses and safe houses) by facilitating regular contact between member organizations and lobbying on collective shelter issues.

Challenges

The five transition houses on the island portion of Newfoundland and Labrador serve a large geographic area which, outside of St. John's, is peppered with small, isolated communities. Essentially, women living in an abusive situation in many parts of the province who are without personal means, have very limited choices: stay in the relationship or leave the community entirely to access services. Transition houses, through partnerships with other government agencies, will provide transportation to get women to shelters for safety, but this is not without its challenges. The difficulty in providing safe spaces for women in rural and remote areas is rooted directly in the geography: communities accessible only by ferry, communities with no police presence, those serviced by poorly maintained roads with no public transportation or taxi services.

In most communities where transition houses are located, no other types of shelters exist: no homeless shelters, emergency shelters or men's shelters. Women's shelters regularly receive "last resort" calls from agencies and individuals who literally have no other place to go but who require services beyond what a transition house is designed to offer.

The situation is more dire and dangerous in Labrador. Shelters and safe houses, particularly on the coast, have to be even more creative in the provision of emergency and crisis services than sister shelters on the island, with even fewer resources.

The problem of inadequate resources is common to all communities in the province, even the largest. While St. John's is the capital city and is often viewed as housing all the resources, demand still outweighs supply. Recent research by the Newfoundland and Labrador Statistics Agency reports that the Northeast Avalon region of the province will be home to almost half the province's population by 2025. Most shelters in the city reach their capacity daily, which continues to put pressure on all services. Transportation, access to programming and treatment all pose continuous challenges in the St. John's region. While public transportation may be available, those seeking shelter often have no money to purchase a bus pass.

Until recently, shelter and other support services provided by transition houses in Newfoundland and Labrador have always focused exclusively and explicitly on women fleeing violent situations. Transition houses were designed to respond to immediate situations of abuse — literally a safe space for women and children to escape violence. Shelter mandates were clear and many explicitly defined the type and source of abuse that qualified women for shelter admission. Women could stay at a shelter if they were fleeing recent abuse from an intimate partner; situations involving a sibling or roommate or a crisis involving historical violence could result in a "turn-away."[1] This practice was established to ensure shelters were keeping their focus squarely on the reason for their existence: female victims of domestic violence.

However, in communities where a domestic violence shelter or transition house is the only gender-specific service providing housing to women, requests for assistance were regularly sought by women in other types of crisis — most notably, women facing a housing crisis. This presented a practical and ethical dilemma for shelters: should they turn away a woman in need even though a bed is available and she has literally nowhere else to go? Does it matter at whose hands a woman experienced abuse?

There is a general understanding that most women who turn up at a shelter have experienced violence at some point in their lives, and experience has shown the vast majority are in the midst of their current crisis (involving housing, mental health, addictions or otherwise) as a result of past violence. This awareness only serves to compound the issue. For many years, shelter staff, keen to help where help was warranted, carefully asked new arrivals the kind of questions in the admission assessment that helped potential clients understand the need to be selective, and sometimes deceptive, in what they shared to gain admission. Thus, shelter rules were circumvented to help more women.

Building relationships with women based on false premises does nothing to establish trust or allow for true supports to occur, and shelters began to deal with this paradox in different ways. Some shelters continued to quietly offer support to women whose needs fell outside strict shelter mandates. Some shelters adhered to their mandates. And some chose to be more overt in their practices, naming the new needs in their communities and vocalizing their intent to meet those needs. The differing opinions and approaches toward women in crisis contributed to serious clashes within the sheltering community provincially. By 2013, the THANL Board began looking at changing the structure of its membership parameters, to limit shelters that provided broader services to associate membership without the same voting privileges.

The challenging conversation happening between shelters was taking place against the backdrop of provincial standard setting. The basic premise that domestic violence shelters serve a very focused population (women experiencing violence) helped form the basis of Provincial Operational Standards for transition houses in Newfoundland and Labrador, which shelters agreed to follow with their government funding body.[2] Unfortunately, as the interpretation of shelter mandates changed and widened in many shelters, individual transition houses were forced to make tough decisions about whether to respond to women in crisis in their communities who fell outside the definition of a victim of intimate partner violence, or violate the provincial standards they had committed to in their service agreements.

Similar discrepancies manifest through many of the philosophies and practices governing shelter work, not just admission policies. Practices involving everything from alcohol and drug use to nightly curfews are prescribed in the rules, then either followed or ignored as perspectives change inside shelters.

Over the past decade, THANL has been through a number of Provincial Coordinators. THANL Board members were as focused on trying to maintain an umbrella organization as they were managing their own transition houses and safe houses. Some of the shelters had new management, which meant the composition of the THANL Board changed. The national conversations about harm reduction and trauma-informed practice were beginning to occur inside violence-against-women shelters in the province. Not surprisingly, conflict began to create change.

Changes

First, the needs of those accessing shelter supports have changed. The number of large families seeking services has dwindled as more women come to shelters without children. It is more common for women living in shelters to speak openly about their struggles with mental health issues, addiction issues, financial constraints and legal concerns than in the past. For shelters to help with the experience of violence, shelter staff must be aware and able to assist with more complex issues than ever before.

As a result, many transition houses in Newfoundland and Labrador are moving toward lowering barriers for women seeking services. While actual practices vary from shelter to shelter (rightfully and necessarily so), there seems to be a common desire to examine current practices and consider changes. The reasons motivating change are numerous but fairly straightforward.

First, responsiveness to community needs remains a foundational value and principle of shelter work. Historically, when shelter staff and boards of directors saw service gaps and unfulfilled needs in their communities, they stepped in to help fill them. This tendency continues, evidenced through an evolution of services over time. In some shelters, this means admitting women with active addictions and providing support even as women continue to use and return to "zero tolerance" shelters under the influence. In others, it means broadening admission criteria to include women in crisis who identify as homeless rather than as victims of violence.

Second, the service gaps for women and families are perhaps better described as chasms in most areas of the province, and this reality is becoming impossible to ignore. Much of rural Newfoundland and Labrador does not have any form of crisis service, outside a toll-free phone number; homeless shelters designed to serve women with needs unrelated to fleeing violence are practically non-existent outside of St. John's; addiction treatment centres are located only in larger cities; lengthy wait lists exist for public housing; and counseling services and thus domestic violence shelters fill many needs in the community.

Third, a burgeoning understanding within community agencies, including shelters, of the lifelong impacts of trauma and violence has led shelters to introduce trauma-informed practices. Work on this issue has been led by Status of Women Councils and other community groups. The work of THANL and Women's Shelters Canada has been important in leading conversations about what shelter work should (and could) encompass. Shelters share the desire to do the best they can for the women and families in their communities and understand that this means adapting to new needs.

The present

Shelters and safe houses in Newfoundland and Labrador have a common root of deep concern for women and families and share a passion for creating safe communities. Navigating the changes in how and to whom we offer support has been difficult within the sheltering community. While each transition house staunchly supports the autonomy of other shelters, conversations about what fundamentally constitutes a "domestic violence shelter" have been challenging.

Some shelters have been resistant to changing their primary mandate — supporting victims of violence — and were concerned about the impact of changes on their clientele. Some expressed concerns that a loss of autonomy for individual shelters could occur if some shelters expanded their focus: might the province then expect all shelters to open their doors on the same basis — forcing some shelters to admit more women than they felt able to serve? Other shelters felt their community issues required a new type of response quickly and believed that the established classification of women's experience of violence created harm where we intended to offer help.

No matter where they fall on the spectrum of linking violence and homelessness, all agree that domestic violence shelters are different and distinct from homeless shelters and must be recognized as such. Domestic violence shelters and transition houses are feminist based, focusing on the unique needs of women and women and children in crisis situations deeply understood by shelter staff. A broad consensus holds that this gender-based approach must be preserved in order to best assist the vulnerable populations these shelters serve.

Using a gender-based approach is the only way to address the differences in how women and men experience violence, poverty and homelessness. These issues are deeply gendered. For example, women's paths to homelessness differ from men's, and their lack of stable housing is more likely to be hidden (through couch surfing, staying in shelters, keeping under the radar so their children are not placed in care, etc.). Women are thus likely to be underrepresented in national homelessness statistics. Not accounting for the gender variance when seeking solutions to homelessness means our response will have different impacts on men and women. As agencies serving women and families, a gendered lens is critical to understanding how violence, poverty and homelessness are intertwined for women so appropriate supports can be implemented.

In March 2018, the provincial government announced that the sheltering program was being moved from the Department of Health to the Newfoundland and Labrador Housing Corporation.[3] This change of government department responsible for administering funds to shelters offers the THANL and individual transition houses an opportunity to formalize the distinction between violence-against-women shelters and other programs, as well as many other needed changes. Operational Standards, service agreements, statistical records, funding arrangements and policies will all need to be revised to reflect the actual practices of our shelters and safe houses. The result, ideally, will be better responses to those experiencing violence in our communities.

The future

The ultimate goal for everyone working on the issue of gender-based violence is to eradicate the need for transition houses entirely. Transition houses themselves play a role in this, of course, although unfortunately the focus of our work is by nature on the after-effects of violence, work that shows no sign of slowing. Ironically, transition houses are stuck in their own cycle of violence as they repeatedly respond to violence but make no inroads toward eliminating it. Most transition houses in Newfoundland have little ability to channel their energy directly into violence prevention work, instead doing what they can to support the advocacy work of their partners in women's centres and the government-funded Violence Prevention Initiative. The entire shelter movement strongly aligns with the principle that "violence prevention is everyone's responsibility."

While optimism for long-term social change fuels our work in transition houses, shelter staff are well aware of the current reality concerning violence against women. As such, shelters continue to seek ways to mitigate harm against women. Essentially, transition houses want to be able to offer whatever a woman or family needs in their time of crisis. This sounds simple but requires many puzzle pieces to snap together: adequate funding and resources; a safe, healthy and well-trained workforce; gender-based policies and procedures that are specific to regional needs but supported in principle and practice by governing bodies; and, last but not least, the continued understanding and support of the communities in which they operate. In this sense, I see transition houses becoming central hubs of support, stabilization, learning, reconnection and healing for women fleeing violence as they prepare to progress in their lives.

Efforts are being made to close the gap between the current role of transition houses and where we'd like to be. For example, at Iris Kirby House, a mental health nurse maintains a presence at the shelter to support women's mental wellness and assist with mental health concerns that go beyond the typical capacity of shelter staff to assess and treat. If all shelters were able to apply this model and expand on it, imagine the positive impact on women and families! In Corner Brook, after thirty-five years operating out of the same aging, inadequate building, a new shelter building has been designed for Willow House so the physical structure is more inclusive and welcoming for women and the broader community. Thought has been given to the physical requirements of a changing clientele and the needs that may present themselves ten or fifteen years down the road. Each shelter in the province has an encouraging story, whether big or small, on change efforts. But what if change weren't so slow?

Willow House's new shelter facility in Corner Brook, Newfoundland.

If the community and government viewed shelters as the centre of a woman's supports as she leaves a violent home, the attitudinal shift would create instant change. There would be no stigma attached to a woman's stay at a transition house. Women would see service providers coming to the shelter and not the other way around. The approach to the provision of health care, legal advice and housing supports would all change. Women who have experienced violence would feel cared for, acknowledged and supported beyond the shelter walls. A woman's feeling of personal safety would continue after she leaves the transition house.

If every member of society understood the capacity we have for violence in our culture and the conditions of inequality that make violence against women inevitable, violence would no longer be tolerated. Attitude forms the basis of violence prevention. In an ideal world, we would be able to nurture the innate quality children possess to want to help rather than harm. Changing the pervasive attitude that violence against women is normal or even okay in certain forms means adults must reframe their beliefs so they can in turn ensure children don't lose their sense of fairness and equality.

We can start with legislating change. Ensure gender balance is targeted and achieved at every level of government. Apply a gendered lens to policy and law. Include women's history and experience in our school curriculum and textbooks. Tackle the wage gap. Implement a national child care strategy that meets the needs of women and families. Spend money on rehabilitating offenders, focusing on real behavioural change rather than pure punishment. Adopt a housing strategy that sees our most vulnerable people safely and securely housed. These actions are limited only by political will. Efforts taken to address root causes of violence will generate huge payoffs. Once our systems and structures are solid and fair, we will notice a decline in violence against women.

CHAPTER 3
Advocacy Centre
Brian Duplessis, Fredericton, NB

November 2, 2007, 8 a.m., second day on the job as Executive Director of the Fredericton Homeless Shelters. As I was having a conversation with a client, a staff member knocked on my door. He said, "Sorry to interrupt you, Brian, but I think Chad is dead on the couch outside your door."

And yes, Chad was dead on the couch three feet outside my office door.

Two days later, a staff member tells me he thinks Freddie and Alfie are shooting up in the bathroom. There were blood splatters on the wall and used needles on the floor. Not exactly a safe-injection site. It was a regular occurrence to find used needles under beds, in beds or just lying on the floor.

Inside the Fredericton Men's Shelter which has been reduced from forty to twenty-five beds through intensive collaboration between various agencies and government programs.

Forty beds plus a few couches in one big room. The beds were two feet apart, and there were two small bathrooms for all residents. There was also a ten-bed women's shelter a few blocks away, which was usually at capacity. Unlike the men's shelter, it wasn't one big room but rather a few smaller rooms that could hold two or three women each.

The men's shelter was located then as now in one half of a building, while another organization runs a community kitchen in the other half — in what used to be the laundry and morgue for the former Victoria General Hospital. The former hospital now hosts numerous non-profit organizations: a detox facility, a mental health clinic and doctors' offices. More importantly from where I sat, it played another role — its large structure successfully hid the men's homeless shelter and adjacent community kitchen from the eyes of the citizens of Fredericton and any visitors who happened to drive by.

In 2007, the area around the shelter was a virtual no-go zone for the average person. Drug dealers were in control, and crowds of homeless men, homeless women and their respective acquaintances would hang out around the parking area (which abutted the shelter) all day and throughout the evening, buying their narcotics, fighting and drinking. We are not talking about kids here; these were Fredericton's crime families. The community kitchen was losing volunteers, many of whom were retirees, because of the constant threat of violence; nurses who worked at the detox centre in the former hospital had to be escorted to their cars when coming off shift at night.

Inside the shelter, there was only one person on staff during the evenings and nights with forty plus clients inside — clients who were dealing with the wide range of challenges that brought them there in the first place, particularly addictions, mental health challenges, family breakdown and poverty. Day or night, the threat of violence was only just below the surface.

How could all of this exist in the picturesque capital city of Fredericton, a small city on the riverbanks of the St. John River? Surely it is an exaggeration. Fredericton isn't one of those big cities with all these kinds of problems.

When I arrived at the homeless shelters in 2007, my first months were consumed with learning about the organization, staffing challenges, funding difficulties and just keeping my feet on the ground. But I was determined that I would get to know the residents as individuals, to understand why they were there and what was needed for them to find their way "home."

I confess that I wanted to take that approach as much for me as for anyone else. I knew I was at risk of not lasting long in the job if I couldn't stay focused on why I was really there. We all need to remember that, after all is said and done, we are not talking about shelters, systems and programs. We are talking about human beings.

In that spirit, throughout this chapter, I want to share a few stories of some of the individuals I had the honour to get to know.

Russell had been at the shelter for several years before my arrival. In January 2010, he presented the worst case I had seen of neglectful treatment by the medical system. He was forty-seven years old when he was severely beaten. He was taken to the hospital, where he was triaged, ignored for hours and eventually wandered off on a viciously cold winter morning, walking about four kilometres to get back to the shelter. He began having seizures, and we called an ambulance. I told the paramedics he needed to be kept at the hospital and treated. Their attitude was appalling, so I also called the ER to tell them he needed to be admitted. I was told very clearly that they couldn't keep someone there who didn't want to stay. I made it equally clear that it would not be acceptable to allow this man to wander off again and die in a snow bank.

His jaw was broken in five places and he was in the hospital for ten days. Oh, I almost forgot to mention, Russell is Aboriginal. Why is it necessary to point that out? Because in New Brunswick the Aboriginal population is just over 3 per cent while the percentage of Aboriginal men and women at the Fredericton shelters was often over 15 per cent.

Two questions

The future of homeless shelters in Canada can be broken into two distinct questions: what *should* the future be for shelters, and what *is the likely* future of shelters?

I don't believe we can talk about the future of the homeless shelter in isolation; that is what we have done in the past. I acknowledge that some shelter organizations have expanded their roles dramatically to provide a variety of services to those who show up at their doors, including counseling, legal help, skills training, detox support and others. Providing diverse and adapted services of increasing quality is fine, but such a focus does not shut off the homelessness tap. In other words, by limiting themselves to being the purveyors of services, most shelters are still not addressing the fundamental, underlying problems of social assistance/welfare systems that seem designed to keep too many individuals in abject poverty — government departments and agencies that don't collaborate and the prevailing view in society that the poor and homeless have inbred moral failings and have brought their state of affairs upon themselves.

One important caveat must be added: there will be no-one-size-fits-all vision for the future of homeless shelters in Canada until the Right to Housing is enshrined in the *Canadian Charter of Rights and Freedoms*. The wide variation between the provinces in income assistance programs, housing support and mental health treatment guarantees that solutions will continue to be stumbling blocks to a national, coherent approach.

I also firmly believe that a discussion on the future of homeless shelters without fully exploring the very need for and purpose of such facilities would be a self-indulgent exercise that serves organizations interested in self-perpetuation and governments who want to shirk their responsibility.

When someone has a physical disability, we build ramps, widen doors, supply mobility devices, provide personal care workers; when seniors need help, we similarly provide care workers, accommodation, deliver meals to their homes and keep them in a hospital at a cost of tens of thousands of dollars a month. But if you have a "moral failing" like an addiction or mental illness, the solution in New Brunswick is to give you $576 a month and leave you in a shelter or on the street.

In this chapter, I will try to lay out this vision of a homeless shelter as an institution that must be a centre that cares for and provides a variety of appropriate services for homeless men and women *and* a place where effective advocacy is carried out to bring about changes to the system that produces homelessness in the first place.

Housing First

On the first half of this twin mission, the half about service provision, let me begin by stating clearly that shelters should operate within a Housing First framework. Housing First is a recovery-oriented approach to ending homelessness that centres on quickly moving people experiencing homelessness into independent and permanent housing and then providing additional supports and services as needed.

I support Housing First — numerous programs in communities of various sizes have demonstrated that using the Housing First approach is beneficial for those involved; it carries the added plus of being cost effective.

We are seeing great progress with community involvement and investment from all levels of government. Fredericton offers a great example of a coordinated effort that has resulted in the municipal government changing from a completely hands-off attitude toward homelessness and shelters to leading a community dialogue and committing funds to construct housing units dedicated to a Housing First program.

However, without housing being enshrined in the

Canadian Charter of Rights, (which is not likely to happen in the foreseeable future), there is a high risk that all the enthusiasm around Housing First will fade when communities realize the flow of homeless individuals doesn't stop.

Shelters should and to some degree are moving to shorter-term shelter stays leading to Housing First, but ambivalence can be seen in local organizations that haven't fully accepted Housing First's basic principles.

What happens when the flow of homeless individuals doesn't stop? Housing First is great for those who are homeless now. But will the community tire, the donors dry up when the flow doesn't stop? Will donors tire?

Housing First is the most critical step of breaking the homeless cycle for individuals involved; it does work and is working.

But there is another cycle it doesn't break — that of abject poverty.

Frenchie — For the first three months I was at the shelters, I saw the name of someone I never met. Frenchie's bed was always neatly made, and he would come in on "cheque day" to pay the nominal rent all residents paid out of their Social Assistance. (This rent was a requirement under Social Assistance rules to prove a person had a real address so they could receive Social Assistance.) A staff member told me that Frenchie was looking after a friend who lived nearby and was dying. The friend could be difficult to deal with so homecare workers were hard to find. Frenchie was in his early 60s at the time, not a very big guy and with no training in homecare. For several months he cooked, cleaned and looked after his friend's personal hygiene. It was only after the friend died that I met Frenchie. When I told him he didn't need to pay his rent for the next three months since he hadn't been there for the past three months, he insisted on paying anyway. He told me that he wanted to pay because he knew the shelters needed the money, and he felt he owed the shelters for saving his life when he needed help. He was at the shelter for about seven years straight.

Where each level of government was/ where they are today/ where they need to go/ what has changed

At the federal level there has been no national plan — the Homeless Partnering Strategy was not and is not a plan. It has sprinkled small amounts of funding across the country for physical upgrades at shelters and funding for a database system called the Homeless Individuals and Families Information System, which is good for gathering statistics but includes no resources to use the management tools it encompassed. New federal funding under the Homeless Partnering Strategy may have a bigger impact going forward as it is now focused on the Housing First model.

At the provincial level, the situation was not much better. There was no funding policy for homeless shelters, only an *ad hoc* annual payment of $60,000 toward the operation of a men's facility and a women's facility, each of which ran around the clock. This sum amounted to 15 per cent of a barebones global budget of about $400,000. The result was one staff person on duty in each shelter at night, most staff receiving minimum wage, untrained staff, and a constant emphasis on fundraising for private donations just to keep the doors open.

Provincial policies on Social Assistance and housing guaranteed that the shelters would be in continuous demand. The introductory rate of Social Assistance up to 2009 was $294, which was applied for six months, after which the person might qualify for the basic rate of $495. Since the cheapest room in a rooming house was $325, the need for the homeless shelter's services was obvious.

The difficulty for the individual needing help was compounded by the need to have an address to get a cheque. The shelters answered this problem — once in the shelter, you had an address — but that meant you also did not have priority access to housing. One caseworker/manager looked after 800 files. All she really could do was verify that clients had an address so they could keep getting their cheques.

Now throw in the impossible waits for addiction treatment. Sure, seven-day detox was available, but it was followed by at least a six-month (often much longer) wait for rehab. The result was detox, followed by detox, followed by more detox.

Mental health treatments were, and in many cases still are, virtually impossible to access. Family doctors are in short supply, which means walk-in clinics and the hospital emergency room are the only services available. That means no follow-up and quite often dehumanizing treatment.

Remember, this was before Housing First was on anyone's agenda.

With the approval of a provincial Poverty Reduction Plan in 2010, a number of positive steps were implemented that had an immediate effect on homeless individuals. Several had a very important impact in a short period of time:

- The $294 introductory Social Assistance rate was eliminated, and the basic rate of $537 applied to all.
- The Household Economic Unit policy was modified so that some Social Assistance recipients would be able to share accommodations without financial penalty.
- Clients of shelters received additional points when assessments were made for housing applications. This started the movement of

long-term shelter clients out of the shelters.
- Additional housing subsidies were made available to organizations that could provide transitional housing.

At the municipal level, the City of Fredericton refused for a very long time to assume any role in the homelessness and housing business. From the way the shelter was hidden from view, an outspoken mayor who had never stepped foot inside the men's shelter despite numerous invitations to do so, the refusal to allow the shelter's management to address City Council and the complete refusal of any involvement for the shelter's funding or operation, it was patently clear that the official position of the capital city was that "housing" and homelessness were not municipal responsibilities.

That willful neglect of "housing" extended to lack of regulation for rooming houses in the community.

However, there has been a striking change in the position and involvement of the City of Fredericton since 2016. With a new mayor and several new councilors, the city undertook a broad community engagement process that has resulted in the City becoming directly involved in the local effort to End Homelessness in Fredericton. While challenges remain, the city has made a concrete and precedent-setting foray into the homelessness space in its 2018 budget with the approval of a direct cash investment in Housing First projects. Leadership truly matters.

How do we know if we are making progress?

In an interesting set of two interviews with Fredericton blogger Charles LeBlanc in 2008, the then local mayor expounded on the issues of poverty and homelessness in his community.[1] His comments reflected the unspoken views of many of the fine citizens of Fredericton at the time.

In the past, the mayor had always been quite consistent in his response as to why the City of Fredericton should not and would not support certain social agencies who were seeking financial support. The basic argument has been one of jurisdiction. However, in the LeBlanc interviews, he said that he wanted to investigate the origin of people using the services of the Fredericton Food Bank, the Fredericton Community Kitchen and the Fredericton Homeless Shelters. He said statistics showed that the vast majority come from elsewhere in the province and across the country. He went on to say that perhaps the reason all these people are coming to Fredericton is because we offer too much support.

Reaction to the mayor's comments from members of the public was predictable. Those who would see themselves as socially progressive were outraged at the mayor's attitude. But the reality is that for the most part, it didn't concern them — out of sight, out of mind.

This clearly is a story of one city at a particular point in time. Every city's experience is different. Even here in New Brunswick, one of the Canada's smallest provinces, the stories from Moncton and Saint John will be unique in some aspects. However, the differences are far outweighed by the common challenges and the need for communities to work virtually as one.

Danny — Sitting quietly on his bed in the middle of the room, legs crossed, eyes down, Danny was easy to overlook when there is turmoil all around. If he wasn't on his bed, he was standing outside in his long coat, summer or winter, with his eyes down. Short walks to the convenience store on cheque day allowed him to stock up on junk food to stuff under his bed or in his locker so he could avoid eating at the crowded community kitchen as much as possible. Nobody knew how long Danny had been at the shelter but everyone knew it was a long time, probably the longest of anyone. Electronic records showed eight years; the Executive Director of the community kitchen thought it was ten to twelve years. When a box of old attendance records was found in a storage room, we found out the truth. From the time he arrived until he was finally placed under Adult Protection and moved to a Special Care Home, it was nineteen years. A nice man. A gentle man, who had been married with a child, was abandoned in a homeless shelter in one of the most prosperous cities in one of the wealthiest countries in the world for nineteen years.

Why won't these improvements end chronic homelessness in Fredericton?

The answer is simple; the solutions are not. Fredericton's recent efforts, combined with those of the provincial government discussed earlier in this essay are laudable. The city is involved, the province is supportive, the federal government is contributing and community organizations are collaborating better than ever. However, homelessness remains an intractable social challenge in the city.

First, homelessness is not geographically limited. Yes, I know I have been critical of the former mayor but one underlying point of his position was that the homeless are coming from elsewhere. He just refused to accept that homeless individuals from Fredericton are equally mobile.

Fredericton, Saint John, Moncton and Bathurst are designated communities under the federal Homelessness Partnering Strategy and thus qualify for federal funding. There is a loose collaboration between the cities, but unfortunately it is very loose. For example, there is no shared database on the clients, no shared counseling or advice as clients move from city to city. There is no team that works in all of the cities to maintain contact and support for the clients.

As it stands, a Housing First client who has difficulty is supposed to receive immediate help and be rehoused as quickly as possible with all the appropriate supports. In New Brunswick, it is relatively easy to move from one community to the other, show up at the local shelter and start all over from square one.

Secondly, as long as Social Assistance rates stay where they are, there will be an endless feedstock for the shelters. We can have long, theoretical discussions and write great theses about the causes of poverty, including multi-generational poverty, but it is all for naught as long as we refuse to address the most basic of human needs — food and shelter. And I defy anyone to meet those needs and look at addressing other challenges in their lives on $576 per month.

I am not going to re-argue the case for a Basic Annual Income. Many others have done so and more effectively than I would be able to do. Instead I am going to share what I have seen from my experience running homeless shelters and from doing intake interviews and counseling at a local food bank.

I want to focus on a particular age group — men and women fifty to sixty-five years of age — only because they make up a significant portion of chronic and repeat users of shelters.

In New Brunswick, to receive the full amount of Social Assistance, a person must have been approved as being "Single with Long-term Needs designation or significant, multiple barriers to employment." In other words, the applicant has to be proven to be highly unlikely to work, especially in one of the poorest provinces in Canada.

If one is fortunate enough to access subsidized housing,

30 per cent of Social Assistance income will be deducted for rent. That leaves $403 per month plus GST/HST rebate of about $50 per month to survive on. Our system makes you exist on that amount which will without a doubt negatively affect your health, both physically and mentally. Then at age sixty-five you magically start receiving $1,455 per month! I have seen many stop using food banks, stop having periodic episodes at the shelter, participating in local activities, treating grandchildren. In other words, on what is still a very modest income by most standards, they are enjoying life.

My question is simple: why are we making people suffer for so long? All the evidence shows economic benefits for society as a whole when we do the right thing.

Third, for the foreseeable future, the opioid epidemic will continue to supply clients for homeless shelters. This isn't something new for those who have been working in the field for any length of time. And it is not deaths that are new but the huge increase in deaths. Over nine years ago, I wrote about the problem in the Fredericton *Daily Gleaner* on this very topic.[2] That's almost a decade ago.

So what is the situation with opioids in New Brunswick today?

According to this story on the CBC, July 31, 2017, worse than ever:

> *Publicly funded opioid prescriptions increased by 28 per cent in New Brunswick between 2010 and 2015, according to the data from the Canadian Institute for Health Information. During that same period, public health plans in the province funded nearly $30 million worth of opioid prescriptions, more than any other Atlantic province. That bought*

more than 760,000 prescriptions — at least one
for every New Brunswicker. Dr. Jennifer Russell,
New Brunswick's acting chief medical officer of
health, has seen charts showing opioid prescribing
trends across the country and said it's "not pretty."

Note that the 760,000 prescriptions are for publicly funded prescriptions and do not include those funded by private drug plans. And none of this includes the human disaster unfolding with fentanyl and carfentanyl.

Fourth, the lack of coordination between government departments and agencies will continue to be an impediment. Yes, they are doing better. There is now some degree of co-operation between the Departments of Health, Post-Secondary Education and Labour and Social Development.

But there are significant gaps. Our justice system fails those living in poverty every day. Legal aid is grossly inadequate and underfunded. Our attempts at utilizing Mental Health Courts have failed through neglect; a proven, successful Mental Health Court was operating in Saint John for ten years but closed in 2013.

Four years later the government got around to reopening the court but again, it was just for the city of Saint John. It is anyone's guess as to when the same service will be available throughout the province.

Terry K was one of several individuals who were at the shelter for five to seven years continuously. All indications were that he was capable of living independently with little or no support. He was in his early sixties when I told him that there was a subsidized apartment available in a seniors building. I will never forget when a few days later he asked to see me in my office.

He sat down and said, "2064123." There was a pause, and he repeated the number. "Do you know what that is, Brian? That is my own phone number. My number."

I asked, "How long has it been since you had your own number, Terry?" With tears falling down his face, he said, "I don't remember."

What should homeless shelters be doing about these pressing systemic issues? What should their role be in bringing about better data management, social assistance reform, reducing the opioid crisis, government service integration and legal aid expansion? They should advocate for it. Shelters need to develop policy capacity to speak on behalf of their invisible clients, who to a large extent cannot speak for themselves. There are no more credible spokespeople than shelter staff members on the topic of strategies that can reduce or eliminate homelessness.

Is ending homelessness and eliminating the need for shelters just a fantasy?

We have so much knowledge of what works, including Housing First, Mental Health Courts, Basic Annual Income.

And we continue to learn from projects such as At Home/ Chez Soi, or the transitional housing projects run by the John Howard Society, which demonstrate significant cost savings for government. But we seem to have no collective capacity for continuing these efforts at the level required. We get a great start, demonstrable results, and then scale back the support.

I think New Brunswick is better positioned than most regions to reduce shelters to simple short-term transitional components of a Housing First program. This would be a proud accomplishment. But it will not happen until governments at all levels make multi-year commitments; until non-profits that provide ancillary supports stop protecting their own turf; until barriers between government departments are really knocked down; until all of the key cities accept responsibility and fully collaborate.

All the pieces are out there: growth of the food security movement; pilots and multiple proposals on Basic Annual Income; Housing First; community willingness.

But, where is the political will to tie it all together? I am not sure it exists.

When we are willing as a society to stand by decade after decade and ignore the fact that more than 140 First Nations communities in Canada lack clean drinking water, then I think the best we can hope for is reducing but never eliminating the need for homeless shelters.

And if that is the case, then perhaps the best we can hope for is homeless shelters that are not stand-alone facilities, feel-good charity programs, run by well-meaning people. They must be professionally run and managed organizations, fully funded by governments of all levels, providing safe, private, clean accommodation; nutritious food; safe injection facilities; detox capacity; addiction treatment and mental health services.

Being pessimistic doesn't mean being hopeless. Look what happened with the change of the municipal administration in Fredericton. Change is possible. But it has to be worked for, sweated for and screamed for. Shelters have to get organized, funded and equipped to do some of the screaming. Present and potential homeless people are counting on them.

So where are they now?

Frenchie — He was one of the first people to qualify for subsidized housing after the introduction of the Poverty Reduction Plan. He continues to enjoy his accommodations.

Russell — Following repeated self-admissions to detox, he reconnected with his home community and relocated back there. I occasionally saw his nephew who told me he was doing very well, including getting back to one of his passions — drumming. Sadly, Russell passed away in August 2017 at the age of fifty-six following a stroke.

Danny — When he moved to a special care home in 2010, Danny had his own room, which he kept spotless. It was discovered that he loved John Wayne movies. He put on weight after he saw a dentist for the first time in decades and had his teeth fixed; he loved treats from McDonald's and going shopping at Walmart. At last report he continues to thrive.

Terry — He is now over sixty-five and awestruck at how his life has changed since he recently started receiving Old Age Security and the Guaranteed Income Supplement. He can now take little trips to visit friends, not worry about his food budget at the end of every month and enjoy a Tim's whenever he feels like it. In fact, I ran into him recently at Tim's, and he insisted on buying me a coffee. What a pleasure to sit and chat with him.

CHAPTER 4
Agent of Social Integration
Matthew Pearce, Montreal, QC

Arrival

I arrived at the epicentre of homelessness in Montreal, the Old Brewery Mission, via Ulan Bator, Jakarta, Lilongwe and Quito. I came to the cause from a liberal arts education and a career in international development education. These experiences had expanded both my mind and my appreciation of causes, effects and challenges of those living with a scarcity of resources, both globally and locally. Homelessness is a condition of scarcity — scarcity of options, of helpful networks and of ready solutions.

When I arrived at the Mission, the depth of my understanding of homelessness, beyond the above, was that shelters represented the high-water mark of services caring for these individuals.

This observation was not only false, but it was also rather

unmotivating. I would have found it difficult to show much enthusiasm for running a service that limited its vision and actions to soothing the hardships of life on the streets. But what I found was an established, well-known homeless institution, which a few years before my arrival had just begun to reimagine itself. It was beginning to transform homeless services in the city, and in so doing have a real impact on the phenomenon and contribute to a genuine reduction in homelessness numbers.

The Mission was moving from being a provider of emergency accommodation to being an agent of social transformation and reintegration. Once that shift was made and embedded into the organization's culture, it was time to review its service offerings in light of its effectiveness at enabling individuals to regain a stable, sustainable and respectable place in their community. When viewing itself as an agent of social transformation and reintegration, the Mission considers homelessness as an episode, hopefully brief, in someone's life.

James' story illustrates the effect of this rethinking about our role in serving the homeless population.

In 2002, James, age fifty-six, came through the Old Brewery Mission's doors. He brought the voices he heard and an unassuming demeanour with him and quietly integrated into shelter life. He was not disruptive and became a sort of shadow among the hundreds of men using our services — spending his days ambling around our parking lot mumbling to himself or to someone others could not see. He was not otherwise remarkable, did not stand out and so stayed on in relative anonymity.

James clearly suffered from an undiagnosed and untreated mental illness. In 2014, he was admitted into our pioneering new program in partnership with the University of Montreal

Hospital's Department of Psychiatry. This program seeks to diagnose and treat mental illnesses among homeless patients and reconnect them with a health care system adapted to meet their needs rather than the other way around.

Traditional health care

Traditional health care delivery consists of an infrastructure — clinics, hospitals, etc. — that we can access if we have carried out the prerequisite conditions the system has laid out for us. The challenge for homeless people is to fit into that system when they face multiple complex barriers and obstacles that differ from those who are not homeless. For example, a homeless person rarely has a general practitioner. This means two things: first, health conditions are not properly or even adequately treated, usually aggravating their severity; second, homeless people tend to resort to hospital emergency rooms when their condition has reached a crisis point for their health care.

When homeless individuals experiencing a serious mental or physical health event arrive at the emergency room, they may need to wait endless hours, as many of us are required to do, before seeing a doctor. This represents an irritation and frustration to those of us who are not homeless, but to people who are, it means that they may miss a meal at their day centre or shelter. They may even miss the allocation of a bed for the night, forcing them to sleep rough outdoors.

They may, especially if experiencing a mental health crisis, sometimes be disruptive and will then be treated with excessive haste, given an incomplete or possibly inaccurate diagnosis, offered drugs that are hoped to have a beneficial effect and a request to return in a week or so to determine if the drug therapy was correct. The individual will often leave the hospital ER, sell the drugs at the door of the shelter and not return for their appointment. This waste of health care services, with its associated costs and lack of beneficial health outcome, led us in search of creative solutions. We realized we needed to adapt health care services for marginalized populations, rather than asking them to continue to unsuccessfully try to shoehorn themselves into a system that did not consider their needs and circumstances.

Using the adapted services developed between the Mission and the University of Montreal Hospital's Department of Psychiatry, after a week and a half of medication and stabilization, the voices abated and James was provided permanent housing, where he remains happily to this day.

And so, we check off another "success story" and move on . . . but the questions remain: Why did it take a dozen years before James received the care he needed? What happened to the Old Brewery Mission between James' arrival and his departure? The two questions are linked.

Origins

The Old Brewery Mission was founded over 125 years ago, in 1889, at a time when people were immigrating to Canada, many landing in Montreal. During this period, people began moving to cities from the surrounding agricultural areas. Both populations were drawn by the lure of wage employment and the promise of being lifted out of poverty that large cities seemed to offer. It worked for many, but not for those who, without the means to afford accommodation and food, ended up on the streets. The growing numbers of people unable to find their rightful place in society represented a public irritation and shame — best kept out of public view.

Caring individuals, often from within Christian congregations, both Protestant and Catholic, responded to this new and growing phenomenon. Their solution was simple:

people were homeless; they needed to be sheltered. They were hungry; they needed to be fed. Other than a few bible readings and hymns, little else was provided.

This model was similar in concept and design to the workhouses that had first appeared in England in the fourteenth century, and which startlingly remained for 600 years — up to the mid-twentieth century. Workhouses were concentrated living environments designed to accommodate and employ those among the sick, infirm and destitute who could not otherwise support themselves. Unsurprisingly, the workhouse concept underpinned both the ethos of the times and the general sensibility about how to handle those who did not or could not fully contribute to economic endeavour or a healthy vibrant society. The context was prison-like, and the point was to render productive a part of the population that was otherwise not.

The initial motivation for creating shelter options for the homeless was charity and compassion, two basic values and tenets of Christianity, amongst other religions. The starting point was that the individuals served were society's misfits, fortunate to be provided for yet often unruly, so in addition to compassion, also necessitating a firm and controlling hand. Although homeless shelter services never adopted forced labour practices, they did incorporate many of the other features that characterized workhouses — concentrated living, tightly packed dormitories, rigid conditions of access and severe penalties for breaches of conduct. The harsh environment and tough treatment found in the workhouses, which often included physical and psychological mistreatment, were not unknown in homeless shelters, despite compassion operating as a primary driving influence.

Throughout the nineteenth and twentieth centuries, homeless shelters became prevalent throughout urban centres across North America and, probably due to their propagation, they became appreciated and valued as a legitimate and appropriate response to homelessness. People no longer needed to sleep on the streets when they could seek accommodation inside a shelter — without charge and usually for an unlimited time. For those who lacked other options and had no family or social support, shelters became home, and no one seemed particularly bothered by this reality. In fact, knowing that homeless people have places to go where their basic needs will be met became (and remains) a source of comfort and a balm to the conscience for the general public. In retrospect, while the homeless shelter solution was certainly based on well-meaning intentions, it was also wrong-minded and misdirected from the start and not in fact a real solution of any meaningful kind.

Shelters were founded on a belief that those using the services were "lost souls," generally unable to be redeemed or function effectively in society. Even those working in the milieu, the front-line volunteers and staff, often subscribed to this notion. Many shelter users were known more by their bed numbers than their names. What had led them to the shelter, the challenges they faced and hardships they endured were the matter of gossip, conversation and compassion. After all, these souls had been abandoned to their fate; they fell beyond the capacity and reach of the formal health and social service system.

Beyond the front line, which often consisted of workers who came from the streets themselves, there was little or no further consideration given to lifting people out of their terrible circumstances. Shelters sought to soothe the hardships of homelessness but did not have, as a central feature of their missions, a vocation of *solving* homelessness. While shelter workers were not blind or indifferent to measures designed to help move people out of homelessness, they had not been selected and hired with solutions in mind and therefore did not normally possess the skill set necessary to work in that way. The skills and orientation required to maintain a peaceable environment, allocate beds, prepare and serve meals, organize showers and clothing changes and generally keep the peace were not the skills needed to assess and evaluate an individual's circumstances and condition nor to help someone establish goals and a trajectory out of shelter life.

Grizzled reverends and street-hardened priests were not uncommon among the shelter leadership. Solid management skills and depth of experience in the social services sphere were far less in evidence. Long-time Mission Director Rev. Bill McCarthy writes in his direct way:

> *We found that we had some less-than-brilliant staff, who could be counted on to do their best to turn things to their own advantage. Some were caught forcing people to take showers as a form of punishment . . . Of course, there is always a risk of letting damaged people try to heal themselves by working with other damaged people.* (The Rev: Memoirs of Montreal's Old Brewery Mission, 1996, p. 39)

This is not to say those running shelters were without sympathy, care or compassion for their beneficiaries. However, with little outside oversight and no regulation, shelter users who had no other support structure around them were vulnerable to arbitrary treatment; that vulnerability was evident in the approach staff employed to maintain a secure environment. Extended and sometimes lifetime suspensions were meted out for various misbehaviours; uncompromising and insensitive reactions to complaints were not uncommon. Shelters did not regard it as central to their mission to offer solutions beyond providing a place to be off the streets for the night. Clients were given a bed and a meal and then after breakfast would be turned back out onto the street until the evening meal in a continual cycle of condensed, regimented accommodation and street life.

While the face of homelessness shifted over the years and continues to change today, the shelter model has stayed intact and largely unchanged. Whether it be immigrants not finding their way, farm workers unsuccessfully looking for paid work in the city, soldiers returning from war with shattered psyches, abandoned alcoholics, victims of increasingly fierce drugs, those struggling with a gambling addiction, mentally ill people who have been "released" from institutions, the shelter remained their only retreat from the streets and their source of both relative security and anonymity.

In recent years, Montreal's homeless population has continued to shift. More young people are finding themselves on the streets, and the city's cultural diversity has become reflected in its diverse shelter population. More women have also come to homelessness and for a range of reasons quite different from those affecting men — abuse and violence, financial vulnerability, mistrust, as well as the mental and psychological strain such stresses inevitably bring.

The shelter model did not properly respond to any of these shifting realities. Shelter workers were, for example, not selected for their cultural sensitivity, and multi-lingual staff arrived by happy accident — not through intentional personnel recruitment.

Shelters had inadvertently become *facilitators of homelessness*; they enabled people who had nothing to stabilize their lives within a state of homelessness. Shelters allowed homelessness to become more than a difficult period in one's life — they allowed it to become normalized as a lifestyle. This is precisely why many still maintain the mistaken belief that for some, homelessness is a life choice. This belief carries the additional benefit of assuaging the guilty conscience — if people *want* to be homeless, well . . . Of course no one dreams of being homeless when they grow up; also it is human to seek structure, stability and security over chaos and fear. Without other available options, shelters provided this firm foundation and, as the number of homeless people sharing the same shelter experience grew, a sort of social support network accidentally emerged within shelters.

"Homeless*ness*" thus described a social phenomenon — a state of semi-stability and permanence on the streets, whereas in a healthy, responsive society, it should instead refer to a temporary tough or trying episode in a person's life, one that is quickly resolved via adapted supports and services.

Warehousing

The shelter, with its human warehousing orientation, was destined to collapse under its own weight. With growing numbers of homeless people and no significant regard for measures to help people escape, society faced the prospect of shelters regularly adding more beds, new floors and new buildings to lodge and feed — towers teeming with the disengaged and excluded humanity within. Tolerance for public disruptions and conflictual interactions among homeless and non-homeless people was being stretched, and a new vision — one that offered relief, reduction, paths out of homelessness — was needed. But who would take on this challenge?

Despite the rapid growth of homeless numbers in most North American cities over the past approximately twenty-five years, the public did not challenge the shelter concept. In fact, it was the opposite. Shelters and their staff received warm praise for carrying out work that others could not imagine undertaking. Today, that praise and appreciation remain. If we were to change not one single element of our original warehousing ethos, we would still be applauded for the magnificent work we do. And it *is* magnificent that low budgets and unpredictable streams of donations did not deter the well-meaning people who kept the shelter doors open, the food prepared and the beds ready. Those who accomplished this feat do deserve praise and acknowledgment. But now we realize that we were not aiming high enough.

Clearly the impetus to acknowledge the errors in previous, and to some extent, current thinking and to reconsider the organization of future services was not going to come from outside the shelter walls — it had to come from within and that, of course, posed a serious challenge. Acknowledging that shelter services — with all their evident benefits of meeting basic needs for those who might otherwise perish — were actually misguided and insufficient was a tough pill to swallow. It took courage for shelter Boards of Directors and staff to admit their institutions were part of the problem, not the solution.

Donors had always responded quickly to appeals to help feed and shelter the needy. How would donors and the general public react to an admission of error from those who had long been regarded as the devoted experts? Would revenues dry up? Why rock a boat that satisfies the public and the donor, not to mention the bulk of the homeless population? Furthermore, how would religious-based organizations reconcile the objective of helping people leave homelessness behind with the notion of gathering and keeping the flock together?

These critical considerations quite naturally gave serious pause to those working with homeless men and women. Nothing short of their organizations' survival was in question. No push was coming from within or without to change and yet, with homelessness continually on the rise, they faced the undeniable moral imperative to admit and learn from a mistaken base of assumptions. If a society regards the phenomenon of fellow citizens living on the streets as intolerable, then those organizations working in the field have an obligation not to tolerate it or facilitate it. If services had been designed to soothe the harshness of homelessness but not to move people out of homelessness in a concerted way, then they were not bold, driven or imaginative enough.

Hard on the heels of this emerging shift in thinking came even harder questions. Where to go from here? What is needed? Do we have the capacity, knowledge, skills and talent?

These challenging existential questions arose in the context of passionate workers and volunteers with access to very limited financial resources, daily confronting the tragic and complicated histories of a clientele largely shunned by the general population. Such a reality often leads people in the field to identify with a sense of distinction — a feeling that they occupy the moral high ground and possess an exclusive and unassailable expertise in their field of endeavour, that they necessarily represent best practices within their sphere. This attitude includes a sense of self-righteousness and strong resistance to criticism from any quarter. Naturally, this type of organizational cultural environment cannot be conducive to questioning one's own practices, let alone honestly reflecting on questions coming from outside.

It must be noted that services rendered to the homeless by community organizations in Montreal came about by evolution and not careful or strategic planning. Needs were recognized within specific neighbourhoods or parts of the city. Responses from caring groups or individuals began to occupy the homeless service terrain over time, with little or no communication or coordination among them. Most of the organizations were and are fairly small in size, scope and scale and thus vulnerable to funding vagaries and unable to have any real clout in government decision-making or in altering public sensibilities. In this context, change represents a threat to a small team of employees and volunteers accustomed to relying on collaboration and solidarity to face daunting challenges and the continual struggle for survival.

Transformation

And yet, if the impetus to transform services does not come from the public and does not come from those working in the field, where will it come from? Are we simply destined to maintain the *status quo*? The impetus will come from those organizations that do not face the challenges of the smaller organizations and that do not struggle daily to survive. It will come from those that operate at a scope and scale that can lead to change — the larger, more established community organizations.

Here is the recipe for progress: the starting point for transformation is to admit into the framework of analysis, strategic thinking and planning an openness and receptivity to constructive criticism, along with honest and transparent self-appraisal. Those who go beyond accepting the need to rethink their actions and services to actually embracing a process for doing so on a regular basis are well on their way. Those who do not will carry on in the manner to which they are accustomed and comfortable; they will provide the same impact and results they have in the past.

When an organization thinks of itself as a purveyor of accommodation, it admits chronic homelessness into its orientation. It permits homelessness to become a way of life. Ultimately therefore, shelters must face the fact that they cannot simply tinker around the edges but rather must face the need for a paradigm shift. The shift? Shelters as agents of social transformation and reintegration rather than providers of overnight accommodation. When that shift occurs, homelessness becomes an episode in someone's life and not their identity.

If shelters accept the mandate to become agents of social reintegration, they must reconsider how they regard their clients and value their potential. Bleak though it may sound, at one time many shelter workers did not truly believe in the capacity of homeless people to improve their lot. We did not fundamentally and profoundly believe in their essential humanity. Dignity and self-realization were not part of the service equation.

Welcoming a guest to the Old Brewery Mission Café in Montreal.

However, as agents of social reintegration, we needed to see them as fellow citizens, as individuals, as people worthy and deserving of our respect and belief in their potential. We needed to learn their names, hear their histories, background and stories, not as gossip but as a means to discern a course of remedial action tailored to their individual circumstances, needs and, yes, desires. We needed to inculcate a deep and abiding belief in their humanity into our outlook, perspective, orientation and practices. In short, we had to think of those who find themselves homeless as anyone else would like and expect to be regarded. Human dignity and mutual respect needed to become service hallmarks, evident in the physical infrastructure and evident in the interactions between staff, volunteers and beneficiaries. From the lost, weak, vulnerable and excluded, people finding themselves homeless become fellow citizens needing help to get back on track to the extent possible, and certainly out of life on the streets.

With this as a guiding force, logically, and abidingly, we had to believe that homelessness can be resolved — that there is a solution for each person who experiences it. We needed to believe there exists a better place and life condition for every person than inside a shelter.

This shift in organizational sense of self and reconsideration of the nature of the problem, as well as the renewed appreciation of our beneficiaries, leads to the next critical step: to lift our heads and look around at what is actually in place and happening elsewhere — regionally, nationally, continentally and internationally. This reflex is not as well developed in Quebec community organizations as it could be, partly due to the language obstacle and partly to an excessive and limiting pride in how we work within our distinct society. We reflexively deny the value of what comes from outside and tend to quickly criticize that which may fit elsewhere but might not in Quebec due to our specific circumstances, whatever those may be. Common wisdom suggests that we do not need outside inspiration or ideas and that we can develop our own path without regard for outside influences.

Of course, this negates the benefit of adapting proven best practices or learning from adjustments others may have made that could help us reduce inefficiencies and time wasted in service development. Montreal is not the only North American urban environment grappling with a growing homeless population. It is illogical to assume then that we can learn nothing of substantive value from the struggles in other cities. Yet such resistance comes not just from community organizations but from the Quebec government itself.

The rapidly spreading Housing First concept provides an example. Under the Housing First approach, homeless people receive rapid access to affordable housing of their choosing, followed by appropriate service supports, all of which enables them to remain sustainably off the streets. Tested and proven elsewhere, and even in Montreal via a federal research grant, the concept was roundly rejected in Quebec as having been summarily planted in the city without consultation. For this reason, the Housing First model became suspect and widely criticized, despite solid evidence that it was effective, and if not less costly than regular services, at least no more expensive and clearly a method that improved its beneficiaries' quality of life. Eventually a *made-in-Quebec* model emerged — "Supported Residential Stability" — which was essentially Housing First with greater latitude as to the range of housing options. The Housing First and Supported Residential Stability models comprised variations on a theme, and the theme was social integration for those otherwise living in social exclusion.

This example highlights two key ingredients for efficient shelter transformation: 1) adapting and implementing promising practices, and 2) using quality data and measurements to feed service design. For too long, the field of homelessness has relied on anecdotes, stories and perceptions rather than data, facts and evidence.

Research

Investment in research increases knowledge and improves the quality of decision making. In 2012, the Old Brewery Mission hired two researchers to work with a lead researcher connected to McGill University's School of Social Work. This team has deepened our knowledge of the profile, reality and needs of our beneficiaries as well as helping us to better understand the impact of services. Its findings have informed service decisions and program modifications.

Early on in the team's work, we learned that fully 75 per cent of shelter users were with us only temporarily and with little or no help from staff would find themselves back on their feet. Another 15 per cent tended to use the Mission services episodically — arriving, leaving shortly thereafter and then returning some time later. Only 10 per cent of all shelter users were chronically homeless — using our shelter month after month, year after year as their home and making homelessness a lifestyle.

These numbers paralleled those of other North American urban centres, indicating that effective practices in place elsewhere could be applicable or at least adaptable to the Montreal milieu. In other words, a benefit could be derived from looking elsewhere and learning from other locations and experiences, not to mention the good news that only about 25 to 30 per cent of all shelter visitors needed longer-term assistance and support.

Further, data showed that the 10 per cent chronic population consumed 50 per cent of shelter resources. This information instantly galvanized our thinking and helped reset our priorities. We realized that we did not need to devote the same amount of resources to each client. If we could attend first to the small but critical group of chronic shelter users, helping them access stable supported permanent housing, we could perhaps unblock the system. We could promote a more dynamic and solutions-oriented approach to service design and simultaneously reduce overall costs by no longer facilitating chronic homelessness. Ending homelessness suddenly seemed much more possible.

To help readily determine the needs of individuals as they arrived, we established a triage residential facility for first-time shelter users, those not already in our database. Offering a three-week maximum stay, including instant access to counseling support, we noted that 75 to 80 per cent left within that time frame. This was not evidence of successful transition support, simply the process of attending to the lighter needs of the temporary population — those who had perhaps broken up with their partner, been kicked out of their apartment, lost a job — who just needed a place to go in the short term while they got back on their feet.

Those who remained after the three-week maximum were offered places in our adapted urban health care or other transition-to-housing programs. The power of solid, academically rigorous research had revealed itself, and there was no turning back.

These researchers are increasingly invited to present their findings at national conferences to share relevant knowledge and approaches. Unfortunately, however, the initiative has not been generalized, receives no public funding and though it has shown tremendous benefits, has not garnered the acknowledgment and appreciation it warrants.

At this point we had opened ourselves to change, accepted the need for wholesale transformation of our services, reconsidered how we viewed our beneficiaries' potential, become data- and knowledge-driven and applied effective best practices. What was next? The hard work.

As an agent of social reintegration, all services would be re-examined, new ones defined and developed. We needed to appreciate that the staff complement required to ensure a secure environment for people to sleep and eat was not the same as that needed to engage with, counsel and accompany people out of homelessness.

Housing

And of course, for social reintegration to be possible, housing needed to be made available. Shelters would be required to convert themselves into purveyors and supporters of affordable housing. We needed to move beyond our walls and learn how to provide ever greater services to clients throughout the community. Mobility and autonomy for staff would become important.

The Old Brewery Mission's new vocation: accompanying homeless people into permanent housing.

The financial resources to achieve this new vocation needed to be calculated, budgeted for, sought and secured. An effort to influence governments was needed for them to understand, appreciate and support a new and more promising direction. The same was true for donors who had become accustomed to and proud of the support they offered to make sure no one was left outside to fend for themselves. As donors have responded appreciatively, increasingly all levels of government have also embraced this new thinking: national affordable housing policies are nearing completion, the Province of Quebec has rallied around the Supported Residential Stability model as a priority and Montreal's municipal government has committed to the concept of ending chronic homelessness.

Large homeless community organizations have coalesced around a collaborative network based on a shared endorsement of this more effective approach; this is evident in their own service transformation. In the spring of 2017, after 128 years, the Old Brewery Mission ceased to offer purely shelter to clients. Now all who come to our entrance are accompanied toward the exit in a supportive manner. Access to affordable permanent housing has become our single largest service offering.

Today, great promise lies in replacing the traditional, long-standing shelter model with dynamic triage followed by rapid transition to housing and accompanying counseling services for those in greatest need — those who realistically will not return to society without ongoing supports. Greater quality of life for clients, a brighter cityscape and an end to concentrated towers of temporary shelters are on the horizon.

CHAPTER 5
The Social Emergency Room
Michel Simard, Trois-Rivières, QC

Leading a shelter

In the early 1990s, I took of a charge of a homeless shelter in Trois-Rivières called Le Centre Le Havre. It was (and remains) a small shelter with twenty-three beds. We functioned like other shelters: a bed for the night and some basic humanitarian services (food, showers, companionship). During the day, people had to exit the facility, but they could come back for lunch. We also developed a rehabilitation program for those who wanted to find a way out of homelessness. These people could stay during the day.

We worked this way for some time, but gradually I became aware that we were not making any progress and that in fact we were part of the problem. Our clients were stuck with nowhere to go, so they stayed. We were always full to capacity and could help very few additional clients. In this context, we decided Le Havre needed to change its trajectory and become part of the solution. It took me some time to develop the clarity of vision to understand how. In this chapter, I will discuss how I became aware of the problem, the path we followed to change course and examine how we can go even further.

How did we become aware that we were actually part of the problem? It happened on two levels at the same time. First, we were facing growing numbers of homeless people who faced increasingly severe mental health problems. Second, we became aware that the shelter experience was not moving anyone or anything forward — neither the people in our care nor the system itself.

Homelessness is a major issue today, but that was not the case thirty years ago. In all of 1992, only 160 men came to Le Havre. Three years later, in 1995, that number had jumped to 360 men. Ten years later, in 2002, approximately 600 people, most of them men, were admitted to the shelter. Twenty years later, in the 2012 calendar year, 1,200 men and women used our emergency services. That's almost a ten-fold increase in demand. How did we respond to the emergency needs of so many people and adjust our services to address these growing numbers? That's the story of this chapter of *Beyond Shelters*.

With Le Havre's complement of twenty-three beds, by 1995 we faced a stark choice: increase significantly the number of beds or find a solution to help people quickly find a way out of homelessness. I chose the second path, and we still have the same twenty-three emergency beds today as we did back in 1992.

Before the nineties, we rarely saw people with severe mental health problems in the shelters. When it became clear that we would have to deal with this new reality, for

which we were not at all prepared, I faced another fundamental choice: adapting our services to the needs and
realities of those persons who fit nowhere or defending
our service limitations and pressuring the public sector to
respond. I chose the first option, but this choice put more
pressure on our emergency services. In the mid-nineties,
around 50 per cent of people in the shelter had a severe
mental health problem. How could we face this challenge
without increasing the numbers of beds and without over-
burdening our staff?

During those years, I tried very hard to find a solution
to these troubling facts. My initial focus was mostly on
individuals with severe mental health problems. I thought it
was possible to help them through program development; I
was wrong. For some years I tried to develop a therapeutic
program that could help people manage their life challenges.
To an extent, this approach succeeded. The program helped
many people live their lives more functionally. I also learned
that accepting one's reality is key to changing it. That's the
paradox of personal transformation and development — we
need to accept reality first, whether we want to transform it
or simply live with it.

More importantly, I realized that the therapeutic healing
process for most people at the shelter, particularly those
with the most difficult problems, was like giving swimming
lessons to someone who is drowning. Shelter residents are
not able to participate successfully because they are simply
trying to survive one day at a time. They certainly needed
help, but before meaningfully engaging in a therapeutic
process, they needed to get out of the water. Today, this way
of doing things is called Housing First.

One day I met a man named Louis. He was about thirty
years old and had been on the streets for a long time,

travelling from town to town. He heard voices and felt para-
noid. When one place became unbearable, Louis moved
somewhere else — that is how he survived. He was a very
private person who kept a low profile and spent his time
alone. One day, he asked me if I would go with him to the
emergency room. He had a serious problem with one of his
feet, and he couldn't walk anymore. We arrived at the emergency room, and we sat there, waiting for our turn in a little
room for people with mental health problems.

A security guard came close and stayed right in front of
us. Louis was terrified. He locked himself in a closet, and he
didn't want to come out. I asked the security guard to back
away so that I could engage Louis. I knocked on the door
and told Louis that the place was safe now. He came back to
the waiting room, but he was nervous.

Louis had a bag with all his possessions. He always kept
his bag with him, everywhere he went; I never saw him
without this precious bag. At one point, a nurse marched up
to Louis and asked him to give her his bag while he saw the
attending physician about his foot. He was literally petrified.
She didn't know it, but she had asked Louis the impossible.
And she insisted and threatened to call the security if he
refused to surrender the bag. That was too much. Louis
couldn't stay, so we left.

Our public systems of care are not adapted for severely
mentally ill or highly complex homeless people. Their options
are jail, the street or the shelter. Louis' experience and others
like it confirmed to me that the traditional way of doing things
doesn't work with people who are not ready, able and willing
to engage in a therapeutic or rehabilitation process. Often the
system doesn't work even when they are ready.

We know that jail is not a good place to help people to
recover from a severe mental health problem, and we know

that the street is not a good place either. What about shelters? Is that the place where the most vulnerable people can find a way out of homelessness, improve their health and regain power over their lives? I struggled very hard with this question because I oversaw a shelter. I determined that we were at least a decent option and certainly better than prison or living rough by the river. At least we offered people a place for the night, meals and access to other services if they wanted. In brief, we were able to welcome people who didn't fit the usual institutions. But in 1995 we still did not offer a solution to the problem. I knew we were still part of the problem albeit not as severe as other components of the system.

Part of the solution

The shift we made was important, even radical. Today, our organization is not based on managing the numbers of beds; we are not a hotel for people who have no money. We need beds of course because people who come to us are bed-less. But the heart of our job is not about managing bed availability for the night. It's about efficiently helping people to stabilize their situation and move them out of homelessness, as fast as possible.

The stabilization process is the focus, while bed management is only a part of this process. Ultimately, the point is not about the numbers of people you can put in beds each night, but how efficiently you can help people stabilize their lives and ultimately get out of homelessness.

A stabilization process is not a rehabilitation process just as a medical emergency intervention is not a rehabilitation intervention. The stabilization process does not require a homeless person to be motivated or committed to personal change in the way a rehabilitation process does. Stabilization requires only the expression of basic needs that the person can't manage by themselves, here and now.

That's how you get the process started. It's not about changing the person, altering his or her sense of self or sense of the world, or even helping them to cope with its reality. It's about helping them to understand their basic needs and then going about meeting those needs. I'll discuss the process we put into place to address social emergency below, but this is the essence of it. Once stabilized through our process, a person then is ready for treatment. And surprisingly, most of them move by themselves to a rehabilitation process. But it takes time and support. And it's rarely a straight line.

An emergency program for homeless people to stabilize them is not and cannot be by itself the solution to homelessness. To be efficient, an emergency service must be part of a system of services, with coordination and direction. Otherwise, all we are doing is managing crisis. The problem is ultimately systemic in nature; the solution must therefore be system-wide, of which the shelter forms only part.

The four essential elements of Le Havre's social emergency program are the following: accessibility, human resources, the process and coordination.

ACCESSIBILITY

The program is accessible 24/7 to homeless men and women. This means that a person can be admitted directly at any moment of the day and can stay during the day. This is not common practice in the shelter world, which usually admits clients in the evening at a specific time and then ushers them out in the morning by a specific hour. Our accessibility policy is more like that of a hospital where, if you are in medical emergency, you can be admitted at any time of day or night and can stay until you are medically stabilized. It's the same thing with a social emergency.

How long can people stay? As I said before, we are not a hotel. So, the answer is related to the speed at which we can address the emergency. We like to say, "as long as it necessary, but as short as possible." While we have no arbitrary time limit, we know that the average length of stay is ten days. If too many clients stay longer than that, we'll run into serious crowding issues and have to turn people away.

THE STAFF

Human resources are key. We have a team working 24/7, always in position to respond. The team is smaller during the weekend and at night, but we are always able to respond 24/7. Staff members are there not only to manage the accessibility of beds, but above all to manage the emergency intervention process. Without a sufficient number of staff with the right qualifications, there is no way to manage this kind of program.

THE PROCESS

The process is quite simple, involving three key steps: 1) assessing the situation and orienting the person, 2) setting targets to meet basic needs, 3) assessing the results. Let's take these one at a time.

First, we take time to welcome the person and help them to understand where they are and what they can expect. Remember, our clients are suffering from an emergency of a social nature. They've lost everything including their relationships, networks, housing, money and usually self-worth. We settle them, collect basic information and help them determine their immediate needs.

Setting targets is the core of the process. The focus is on the needs of the person, here and now, and the targets that we can manage in the context of their situation, their motivation and the direction the person wants to take. We work to find the best strategy to meet the clients' needs, especially housing, treatment, money and outstanding judicial issues. The targets represent what we have to reach to stabilize the person, help him or her out of their immediate emergency situation and direct the individual ultimately out of homelessness.

As I've said, this process is not about changing the person or requiring that he or she take immediate responsibility. Rather, the goal is to help the person develop the best strategies to meet their needs and stabilize their situation. Housing is almost always the first target, but this can vary based on the person's circumstances. We must listen carefully to discover the most appropriate targets.

It's very important to make the distinction between emergency programs and Housing First programs; they are not the same. The first leads to the second. Stabilization can lead to Housing First. So, we try to include Housing First in our target-setting where appropriate and coordinate Housing First programming for clients who have been stabilized.

COORDINATION

This is essential. The team must work together and have access in real time to all the information that is needed to manage the process. We have developed sophisticated computer-aided tools to structure the process and share the information with every member of the team. It works very well because, frankly, it must work well. You can't manage an emergency service with large flows of people in a place with limited resources without an efficient information system. That's the way to coordinate the team and manage the service.

Developing permanent solutions out of homelessness

In this way, we transformed Le Havre into a social emergency centre. But we went further and actually developed housing for our clientele and created a workforce development agency to help homeless people learn useful employment skills.

First, we created a non-profit organization to develop permanent social housing units, relying on provincial funding, and other types of housing units with the help of federal and private funding. Rapidly, we were able to build large numbers of units for homeless people in Trois-Rivières. At the same time, we continued to develop mechanisms for our clients to access private- and public-sector permanent housing. In this way, we created a wide and robust gateway out of our emergency program, thereby sharply reducing the growth of chronic homelessness in our community. This was also the key to keeping the number of beds in Le Havre relatively small.

We also created a non-profit organization to develop workplace skills for our clients. Right now, we have five sites with more than 250 people working in different projects and at different levels. Attachment to the workforce can be a powerful antidote to despair and give formerly homeless people the opportunity to have a life, not only a place to live.

There's one more key piece to puzzle and that's how we worked with public sector and non-profit institutions.

Developing a system of services

One of the problems we faced was fragmentation and competition between the agencies serving homeless people. We realized that the clients and the precarious circumstances in which they found themselves could not be managed by any one agency alone. We needed to figure out how to bring integration, coordination and oversight to our collective services. In other words, we needed to find a way to work together.

To do this, we worked on two levels. First, a task force was set up to figure out a strategy to solve the systemic problem and meet the needs of homeless people. This task force was composed of people who have decision-making power and could implement an integrated system of support. The task force gave birth to an interagency structure with a united team entirely made of staff from the different partner organizations, including police, social work, addiction and drug treatment, housing, employment services and several others. Based at the Le Havre, this outreach team has three mandates: case management for homeless people coming into the shelter, coordination of services and maintenance of a collaborative culture between agencies.

This team constitutes a sort of flexible Housing First program, focused on the most difficult situations. It has direct access to housing services, treatment and employment

Centre Le Havre: the Social Emergency Room in Trois Rivières.

skills programming. The team focuses on safe exits from the shelter. It has even developed an adapted health pathway for homeless people with seamless access to medical emergency services. A diversion-from-incarceration project for persons with mental health and judicial problems has also been developed.

Looking forward to ending homelessness

At the root of La Havre's transformation from traditional shelter to social emergency program within a network of services and programs was our commitment to ending homelessness in Trois-Rivières. So how have we done?

Today we manage up to 1,200 clients each year with the same number of beds that we had back in 1992 (when only 160 clients requested our services). We made it possible because the length of stay in the shelter dropped dramatically. We stopped warehousing homeless people and started building efficient and sustainable ways out of homelessness through permanent housing and work.

We've housed a lot of people over the last almost twenty years, and I cannot imagine what our city would be like if we hadn't. We also know that lot of people who were homeless for a long period of time whom we helped to house are still in their homes. They landed in permanent housing after going through the process of our social emergency program. But we haven't eliminated homelessness, and we know that we have a lot more to do.

We also know that troubling facts still exist. The number of newly homeless people in our region continues to grow, and their situations and condition remain very difficult to manage. We'll keep working in the way we are, but if we want to go further and reduce the phenomenon seriously, I believe we must develop a broader and more comprehensive vision of homelessness. We need another shift — this time from the systemic level to the societal level.

We have to be aware that homeless people are not born in the streets and that the phenomenon cannot be understood outside the core of the society in which it is appearing and developing. We cannot address this problem at the level of the services and programs only. We need to focus on choices that have a structural impact on the global development of our societies.

Homelessness as a societal problem does not arise because of insufficient services and programs, just as suicide or addiction are not produced by a lack of services and programs. But if we don't have adequate and sufficient services and programs, and the right vision and approach to tackling these human and social problems, we will never actually defeat homelessness. In other words, we have to develop a vision for preventing homelessness in the first place. Until we choose to implement policies that make society fairer in general, more equal and more affordable, the troubling facts of homelessness will still be with us and confront us every day. Shelters and their partners will try to hold the fort until those better days arrive.

CHAPTER 6
Homes, Jobs and Friends
Dion Oxford, Toronto, ON

I was born in rural Newfoundland in 1969 — the same year that the Rolling Stones released one of their most famous songs, "Gimme Shelter"; this became somewhat of a mantra for the work I've done throughout my career.

Having grown up in the Salvation Army, I was exposed to music from my first breath. Early on in my life I became a musician and a strong believer in all that the Salvation Army represents. At twenty, I quit university after concluding that I absolutely did *not* want to pursue math and science as a career, grew my hair long, pierced my ears and moved to Toronto to chase my dream of becoming a rock star!

That's when things really began to change for me. The rock star life wasn't cutting it financially, so I needed a real job to pay my bills. Through church connections, I was hired as the cook at a Sally-Ann drop-in centre for folks who were homeless. That changed my life forever.

I quickly learned that my idea that I would "save" the homeless clientele was completely wrong-headed — I was the one being saved. The richness of the relationships that I was privileged to form with folks on the street was overwhelming. I learned lessons about life and love, good and hard things, forgiveness and grace and gratitude and surrender. My life was being changed, and I decided that I wanted to spend the rest of it doing this work. Since then, I have worked among people on or close to the street in several different capacities, including founding and operating a shelter for close to fifteen years, all with the dual desire of seeing lives changed and having my own life positively altered along the way.

If I imagine shelters ten years from now, I mostly hope that there won't be any — because the need will have disappeared. No one should be without a home. There is more than enough of everything to go around. Even one homeless person is too many!

Having worked alongside homeless men and women for many years, I have learned a lot about life, love, community and hope. The people I have been privileged to meet and befriend on the streets have been my teachers for a long time. I have learned that everyone is different; every human being is unique and brings unique needs and gifts. All people have something to offer this world, no matter where they live, how much money they make, their race, gender, age or religion.

Sometimes people are homeless because they actually don't believe they have skills to offer the world. They have been taught to think of themselves as needy, as perpetually needing help, as a drain on society. No one has asked them what they can give. Society has created dependency by only viewing them as the recipients of services or programs.

I believe that as part of the campaign to eliminate homelessness, shelters need to ask the questions, "What can you give?" "What are you good at?" "What gives you hope?" "Where do you want to go in life?" "What can we do to help you get there?" This will spark true healing in the lives of shelter users and help them on their unique journeys out of homelessness. By helping homeless people answer these questions, we allow them to discover or rediscover their purpose and move from survival to truly living.

To successfully answer these questions, people first need three key things:

1. a home,
2. a job and
3. a friend

If all Canadians had a home, a job and a friend (or two), we would have no need for homeless shelters. People would have enough of everything they needed. In fact, all of us would have abundance, or at least enough to have a good life.

Poverty in our first-world context is not one of material things. Rather, poverty results from greed. Poverty leads to isolation and fear, which in turn creates loneliness, which can then lead to any number of conditions such as addiction, violence and homelessness. The answer to our problems does not involve finding more money. It is about finding the strength, the courage and the will to do things the right way and to stop offering short-term and inadequate solutions once and for all.

Below I try to outline how shelters can play a constructive role in accompanying homeless people on the journey to having these three basic human requirements — a home, a job and a friend.

A home

First, we must recognize that "housing" is not the same as "home" but also that "home" is not possible without "housing." Home starts with housing. When people don't have a place to live, a place to call their own, with all of the rights and responsibilities that come with having a dwelling, the goal of recreating the house as a home is illogical. We need to find housing first.

"Housing First" is *the* program that rules the day in the shelter/homeless world. After close to thirty years in this work, I confess that I am a convert to this idea — on paper. There are actually two competing versions of the Housing First model. Under the politically driven model, people experiencing homelessness are often placed in less-than-suitable housing for the sake of the statistic — to prove, for example, that the relevant city's ten-year plan to end homelessness is working. Suitable housing means the dwelling is big enough, hygienic enough and permanent enough for the new tenant to want to stay there for a long time. A transitional unit (e.g., housing designed for a one-year period at most) that is poorly maintained and the size of a shoe box may technically amount to housing, but it's really not anything near a home.

Then we have the model that does its best to find suitable, affordable, durable housing for homeless men and women. This latter version of Housing First — the harder but better path — requires patience and tenacity as there is far too little housing stock that matches these characteristics. To qualify as affordable, the formerly homeless person must pay no more than 30 per cent of their income toward rent (which usually means 30 per cent of their welfare cheque).

Clearly this latter model requires an advocacy component, working to expand and improve available housing stock. At the end of the day, Housing First only works if there is actually housing. To this end, shelter staff typically attend every table and committee meeting possible so as to speak loudly and in a unified way about this critical need. Explaining to politicians, senior provincial bureaucrats and city officials that our shelters are and will remain full until suitable and affordable housing is built comprises a vital piece of our work.

In my Christian faith tradition, I have read quite a few parables in which Jesus talks about the difference between houses built upon solid foundations as opposed to those built on sand. Houses built by smart carpenters on rocks stand firm when the winds and the rains come, but those built on sand by people who cut corners to save time and/or money just crumble away when things go sideways.

I understand that these stories are meant to be interpreted as general life lessons as opposed to literal messages about housing, but they nevertheless contain a lesson pertinent to the Housing First model: we simply cannot continue to place people in housing that is not suitable and not affordable. People in such housing will attempt to stay but will eventually be driven out because the unit is too small, it isn't permanent, there is too much drug dealing in the building, the rent goes up without notice, there's no electricity or heating in the apartment or any of a hundred other reasons that makes the dwelling basically unliveable.

What do these people do then? They come back to shelters; I've seen it countless times. We will continue to encounter this phenomenon social workers call "recidivism" (repeated experience of homelessness) if we don't start making sure that the housing to which we connect people is built upon a solid foundation and not just "shifting sand."

Again, the first step is to ensure that good, solid housing gets built or otherwise made available. Currently, homeless people face waiting lists that often are many years long for a decent dwelling. This leaves them little choice but to go on living in shelters or in cheap, bug-infested apartments run by slumlords who only care about the dollars. Some housing is being developed, but not nearly enough to keep up with the need.

Once the housing piece is resolved, we can explore what else is needed to make a home. When I asked homeless people using shelter services what components besides housing make up a home, they gave me some incredibly insightful answers. While we do our best to create a "home like" environment, shelters are simply not designed for long-term living. Here are five things that we must consider in our quest to create permanent homes:

Safety/sanctuary

People need to feel safe to be at home. Having to constantly maintain vigilance over one's person or possessions creates a sense of edginess and concern that does not allow one to relax — ever! The ability to lock one's door when leaving or entering one's place is necessary for someone to feel safe. People need to know that no one can come or go from their space without their approval; this gives them a sense of safety for both themselves and their things.

That sense of safety allows the space to become a sanctuary — a sacred place, where someone can go and feel safe from harm. This allows people to let down their guards, meditate, relax and focus on who they are as a human being.

We who build and operate shelters do our best to ensure safety for everyone present, but with one hundred or more people residing together in one place, safety concerns cannot be eliminated. As good as our shelters may be, they are no place for someone to settle into or live in permanently. They simply do not and cannot offer a true sense of home — for anyone. All people deserve more than that. A place of safety/sanctuary allows a person to focus not just on their personal well-being but on their emotional/psychological health as well.

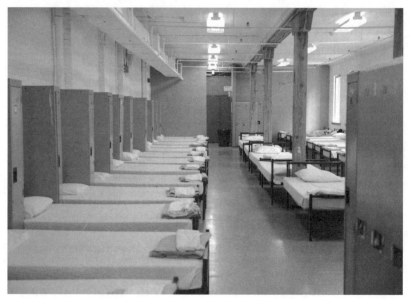

Inside the Gateway Shelter in Toronto.

Security

With respect to security, I'm mainly referring to some basic elements that most of us take for granted, such as food and income. If someone is worried about where the next meal is coming from or how he or she is going to pay the rent at the end of the month, that person will never have a sense of being home. Ensuring that everyone has enough to both pay the rent and buy the food they choose to eat is crucial in our pursuit of home-ness.

Freedom

Again this sounds very basic and refers to something that most of us take for granted. But when someone has the freedom to come and go as they please, to go to bed when they feel like it — whether that's in the middle of the day or the night — to eat the food they want to eat, when they want to eat it, that person is home. The same is true for the freedom to have any guests come by that they choose, for as long as they want, to own a pet, play the music they want to hear, take a shower when they want. These things represent that sense of freedom that leads to a sense of home.

Comfort

It's really nice to be able to put your feet up on whatever it is you feel like putting your feet up on, turn on the television to whatever show you want to watch, go to bed on whatever type of bed you chose to buy, use the pillow that you've decided works best for you, wear whatever you want to bed or nothing at all if you prefer, get up whenever you feel like it, take a shower using your preferred soap and just lounge around the house as you so choose. That is comfort! It truly does not and cannot exist like that in a shelter no matter how hard we might try. All people need comfort to have a home.

Community

People like to know their neighbours. They like to know they have things in common with others who live nearby. People need to put down roots in the neighbourhood, all of which takes time, patience and sometimes the kind of help a shelter can offer. For this reason follow-up programs that help people connect with community resources — the library, softball team, knitting club, local places of worship, courses, cultural or other events — are vitally important. Our shelters now have staff whose entire job involves community follow-ups. When someone moves out of our shelters, this person helps connect them to local community supports, advocates for them if things don't go according to plan, joins them for meals and a little socialization and generally keeps in touch. Sometimes folks who have been socially isolated need help connecting to the neighbourhood. With supports in place, a sense of being part of a community develops and the housing starts to feel like a home.

A job

Sometimes we view our jobs as a curse. Getting up every day and doing the same things can get boring. We begin to count the days until the weekend. However, I view a job as a genuine gift. A place to go where we can use our skills and then be rewarded with meaningful pay is nothing less than a blessing. Meaningful work for meaningful pay is so important for every individual. Regardless of abilities or health challenges, everyone has the opportunity to feel important and valued when they have work.

First, we need strong and consistent advocacy to change our societal mindset from the idea of a minimum wage to the healthier concept of a liveable wage. The very concept of minimum wages suggests that this is the least amount of money that an employer must pay an employee to avoid breaking the law. People deserve to be paid at least enough to have a decent living. While the issue involves complexities and nuances, we can work toward a societal consensus that it is simply not OK for people to work and not make enough money to pay for life's necessities.

Of the three topics under discussion, we pay least attention to the *job* piece when it comes to addressing homelessness. We do this because we assume that either there are no jobs for homeless people or homeless people cannot work or be trusted to work. These assumptions are not entirely untrue. Work in general is becoming more technical and requiring more qualifications and credentials than many homeless people have attained. Homeless people also face a great many barriers to employment, not least of which is lack of housing. One cannot work regular hours for very long while living in a shelter. In addition, many homeless people are dealing with both acute and chronic health conditions.

Nevertheless, much can be done in the area of employment for homeless people. Opportunities exist in areas such as auto mechanic work, including oil and tire changes; locksmithing; elevator maintenance; food services; garbage and waste disposal; construction and hotel services. How do we link homeless people to these opportunities? One answer is to create social enterprises — businesses designed to hire and/or train difficult-to-employ people. Many shelters like the Gateway (as I'll discuss below) have introduced social enterprises as a training ground for the men and women they serve. Other shelters are hiring employment specialists to help retrain their residents and connect them with potential employers.

The Hebrew language has a word, *raeb*, that describes someone who is poor because they are experiencing famine. They get up every day, till the soil and water the plants and do everything right, but at the end of the season it either rains too much or too little, is too hot or too cold or for some other reason they do not yield any fruits of their labour.

Our culture is witnessing an urban famine. People get up every day, they look for work, they do everything right but reap no results from their labour because so few available jobs pay what they need to have a decent living for themselves and their families. Our response has to be creating social purpose enterprises.

When I was operating a shelter for the Salvation Army in downtown Toronto, the Gateway, I realized we were paying $50,000 annually to a local laundry company to clean all our bed linens. I also recognized that we had many people living in our shelter that wanted to work. After consulting with the other four Salvation Army shelters in Toronto, I learned that all together we were spending hundreds of thousands of dollars every year for laundry services.

Why not open our own industrial laundry facility and train the people who live in our shelters to operate it? This is what we did — a laundry social purpose enterprise that we called Gateway Linens. Now our facility does all the laundry for all the Salvation Army shelters in Toronto, and we have eight or nine contracts with other Toronto shelters and drop-ins.

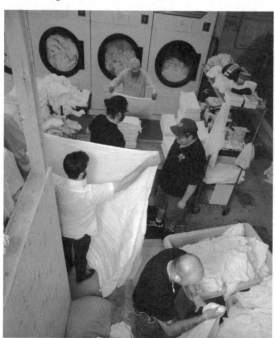

Gateway Linens in operation: an innovative approach to programming in a homeless shelter.

We have developed a partnership with a local laundry company, under which people who graduate from Gateway Linens who want to stay in the laundry business are guaranteed a full-time job with the potential for unionized pay and benefits. Gateway Linens is one of many social purpose enterprises across Canada in response to the need for all people to have a job. These go a long way toward home-making.

A friend
The kind of poverty we see in Canada is quite different than what we might witness in a developing country. Our poverty is often not just a material-based issue but also one involving a lack of friendship. Anecdotally, during my two decades of working in shelters, almost all the people experiencing homelessness that I have encountered have told me that one of the major problems they face is social isolation: loneliness.

Friends are hard to find and friendships take time to cultivate. While most of us take friendship for granted, many people who live in shelters have no real friends they can lean on. How do we help someone who has shared with us how deeply lonely they are to create a true sense of home?

The answer is obvious. People from the streets and shelters have told us in no uncertain terms that they need and want friends. Therefore shelters need to connect people to others whom we think might potentially become true friends over time. Causeway, an initiative of the Salvation Army shelters in Toronto, attempts to address this problem. The program intentionally connects members of local communities with people who were recently homeless but are beginning a new life in a neighbourhood. The purpose is to build unlikely yet mutually beneficial friendships.

The idea for Causeway came from an awareness that many of the men and women who leave shelters and find housing end up feeling isolated and alone in their new apartments. Ultimately, many lose their housing for one reason or another related to that loneliness. They end up back in the shelter system because it's the closest thing to "home" they know. When staying in our shelters they have community, but when they move into their own apartments, they are all alone with no friends or family and no idea of how to begin finding or building community in their neighbourhood.

Meanwhile, many caring everyday people regularly ask, "How do we get involved?" Many people really want to do something more than just write a donation cheque. There is a stirring in people's hearts and souls to do something about injustice and poverty, but they're unsure what form that might take while they have jobs and family responsibilities. They want to roll up their sleeves and help but don't know where to start.

Causeway addresses both of these realities. In fact, the word "causeway" comes from the concept of bridging a gap. A causeway is a person-made bridge between two previously separated and impossible-to-connect bodies. The bridge that the Causeway Initiative is trying to create is between rich and poor, between people with resources and people who lack them, between local neighbourhoods and shelters, between people who have community and people who desire it.

Causeway is *not* a social service program. It is not about providing "services" to "clients." It is an initiative that can only work if both parties understand that the friendships being created can and will be mutually beneficial.

The Causeway initiative is based on the belief that, while there are not enough "professionals" to provide follow-up supports to individuals being housed, there are more than enough committed people all across Toronto that could. Causeway offers an avenue for people to respond to the problem of loneliness and of homelessness in practical and vital ways.

Once we have a critical mass of potential volunteers, we conduct training sessions for them with topics like friendship building, boundaries, risks, social determinants of health and well-being, potential outcomes and measuring success. When we have trained volunteers, we will match them with people who express interest in having Causeway volunteers walk alongside them after they have been housed.

The housing specialists will ask each person they house whether they are interested in having a pair of volunteers from the Causeway Initiative visit them after they have moved into their apartments. If they express an interest, we will invite the trained Causeway volunteers to a meal to meet with the housing specialist and the individual moving into the community — the start to the relationship. The Causeway Initiative invites people to join together to "walk the walk" with individuals who have recently experienced homelessness. The road to healing is often frustrating, and those beginning the journey need a friend to guide and encourage them through the obstacles they will face.

This initiative is developed to encourage compassionate people to develop "unlikely friendships" by providing presence, guidance and support. Caring community members can help ensure a positive and successful journey for individuals who are beginning their walk toward wholeness.

When these two groups come together, they learn that they both have something to offer each other. People who are poor receive a friend as well as help in connecting to the community and its resources. Also, their stereotypes of "the rich" begin to be broken down in the context of friendship.

People who appear to have everything they need and want realize that their newfound friends, who seem entirely needy on the outside, have riches to offer their friendships despite, and often because of, their poverty. Their stereotypes of "the poor" also begin to dissipate over time in the context of friendship. Their new friend's insights into life, love, relationships, community and God are often profoundly rich due to their life experiences. Ultimately, the hope of Causeway is that everyone involved will learn that they need each other.

Similar programs are springing up across the country, based on the understanding that friendships form an essential aspect to creating "home-ness." These programs bring members of the general public — people with everyday lives working in everyday jobs — into close contact with folks moving out of our shelters and offer them a platform to build friendships, which then help break down myths and stereotypes. Relationships built on real life interactions and experiences break down walls and lead to real friendships, which then help create true home for everyone involved.

If we focus on these three simple things — a home, a job and a friend — we can end homelessness as we know it. If we as a society can truly treat people like people and not like projects to fix, we could see real and lasting change throughout towns and cities everywhere. In the meantime, we still have a lot of shelters in every major city across this country. Tens of thousands of people in Canada still have no place to stay each night except a shelter.

Our goal must be to put ourselves out of business. Everything we do, every program we create and operate, has to be focused on getting people off the street, out of shelters, and into their own homes. If anything we do serves only to maintain homelessness, we must stop and change our focus. Shelters are morally bound to work toward their own elimination. Thus, they should all be compelled to advocate for, promote and practise finding homeless people a real home, a real job and a real friend. It's as simple as that.

CHAPTER 7
Youth Prevention and Early Intervention

Tammy Christensen, Denisa Gavan-Koop and
Kelly Holmes, Winnipeg, MB

"I know about youth homelessness. I know that it is not a choice. It affects your self-esteem and your worth. You do not feel like you belong, and sometimes you stand out more than others. You can make bad choices when you are homeless, like prostitution and crime. You have pressures when you are on the street, and you learn to do drugs."

— Savannah, Youth

Early on a cold and dreary morning in Winnipeg, a couple of youth were standing along Portage Avenue, one of downtown Winnipeg's busiest streets, asking for support for the West End 24/7 ("WE 24/7"), a safe space for youth. It was 2015, close to the holiday season. They were hoping to capitalize on the generosity that Winnipeggers are famous for around this time of year. *"Honk for Coffee in Support of the West End 24/7 Safe Space for Youth"* one bright yellow sign read.

These young people were braving the cold and handing out coffee for spare change for a very serious reason. Over the course of several years, Winnipeg youth, many of them Indigenous, had gone missing, been sexually assaulted, exploited or had died tragically. This prompted numerous calls to action focusing on early intervention and prevention. The community — and youth-oriented organizations in particular — clearly needed to be able to give vulnerable young people the supports and services they needed before they found themselves in unpredictable and unsafe circumstances. To accomplish this goal, youth need safe spaces when home is no longer a refuge.

The concept of 24/7 youth safe spaces is not new to Winnipeg. Rossbrook House was the first youth safe space created in the Centennial Area in 1976, and every subsequent youth safe space has borrowed and adapted components of that model. Rossbrook House was a community initiative that aimed to offer young people refuge from the destructive environment of the streets and to divert them from involvement in the criminal justice system.[1] Every community-driven initiative to create youth safe spaces has focused on one goal — keeping Winnipeg youth safe and alive.

The death of Indigenous youth in 2007 and 2014 led to the creation of the Sexually Exploited Youth Community Coalition (SEYCC) and Ndinawemaaganag Endaawaad Inc. (Ndinawe) youth safe spaces. Ndinawe provided support and services to youth in the Winnipeg's North End but struggled to maintain funding until recently.[2] SEYCC created a network of Winnipeg organizations and community members working together to address sexual exploitation in Winnipeg.

The need for a youth drop-in centre in the city's West End gained momentum in the fall of 2014 after the tragic death of an Indigenous youth. Witnesses reported seeing the young woman in the West End prior to her death. The Spence Neighbourhood Association (SNA) had been running a youth drop-in program from the Magnus Eliason Recreation Centre, a city-owned community recreation facility, but it was not open twenty-four hours, seven days a week. If it had, maybe it would have provided her with a safe place and access to necessary resources and supports.

Youth workers at SNA were growing frustrated at turning youth away late at night: "We found that we were pushing kids out at 9:30 p.m. That's when the doors close; there's no other place for them to go. It's dark, they're vulnerable and there's a lot of resistance in our youth."[3] Over the course of a couple months, SNA managed to raise $25,000 to fund two positions for a 24-hour drop in space for West End youth in crisis or with nowhere to go.

Although the initial funding got WE 24/7 off the ground, SNA currently struggles to keep its doors open. The youth safe space received funding from January to March 2018 as part of a city-wide Cold Weather Strategy, but funding for the next winter to keep WE 24/7 open remained uncertain.

Many youths who do not feel safe at home resort to couch surfing in the homes of friends or extended family. Others resort to more risky types of housing involving prostitution or rough sleeping. They are at a higher risk of being exploited, raped, assaulted, or exposed to the cold Prairie weather. A homeless youth is a youth whose life is at risk.

Every day, at least 200 youth in Winnipeg have no place to call home.[4] Youth are the fastest growing segment of the homeless population in Canada.[5] They are part of the hidden homeless and among the most vulnerable. Youth safe spaces are specifically designed to meet the needs of young people and connect them to a variety of supports and resources, such as accessing housing, mental, physical and sexual health support services, clothing, employment services and food. These safe spaces function as an emergency response for youth. Excitingly, they are also fundamentally shifting the response to youth homelessness through planned, supported and healthy transitions and offering both prevention and early intervention strategies.

This chapter will describe the Winnipeg landscape and how the environment and demographics have shaped specific strategies to combat youth homelessness. It will also present a definition of youth homelessness, describe pathways into youth homelessness and provide context to what is happening "on the ground" through Winnipeg-specific data gathered in the 2015 Winnipeg Street Census. This culminates into a discussion about the spark that led to Winnipeg's first youth homelessness strategy and how youth service agencies are shifting the youth emergency response to prevention, early intervention and supporting planned and healthy transitions out of homelessness.

The Winnipeg landscape

Winnipeg is located where the Assiniboine River meets the Red River. It is Treaty 1 territory — the original lands of the Anishinaabe, Cree, Oji-Cree and Dene peoples and homeland of the Métis nation. Manitoba has the highest number of Indigenous people of any province at 195,900, representing approximately 14 per cent of Manitoba's total population. Approximately one in seven Manitobans identify as Indigenous. Winnipeg has the highest Indigenous urban population of any major city in Canada.[6] Approximately 98,810 people in Winnipeg identify as Indigenous, accounting for 12.2 per cent of the total population.

There are several promising facilities in Winnipeg that provide emergency response services to youth experiencing homelessness. Rossbrook House, Ndinawe and SNA's WE 24/7 all provide safe spaces for youth who have nowhere to go. However, all three have been plagued by inconsistent funding at one time or another. Ndinawe also runs a youth emergency shelter (sixteen beds up to the age of twenty-one), as does Macdonald Youth Services (eight beds generally for those twelve to seventeen years old). Adult emergency shelters include the Salvation Army and Siloam Mission (eighteen years old and up) and shelters that provide refuge to victims of domestic violence, such as Willow Place (eighteen years and older). RaY (Resource Assistance for Youth) also provides emergency safe suites for youth exiting Child and Family Services' (CFS) care (seventeen to twenty-one years old).

The 2015 Winnipeg Street Census was the first-ever attempt at establishing a comprehensive view of homelessness in Winnipeg. The census provided a "moment in time" snapshot of youth homelessness to better understand how many youth are experiencing homelessness and why youth are precariously housed, couch surfing, seeking shelter in youth safe spaces or sleeping rough on the streets.

The census found that youth between the ages of sixteen and twenty-nine made up 26.5 per cent of all people experiencing homelessness.[7] While the census could not capture data on hidden homeless youth, they were able to collect the data below, which presents alarming portrait of youth homelessness in Winnipeg:

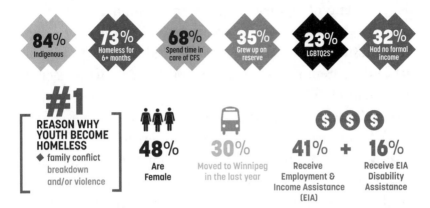

A "moment in time" snapshot of youth homelessness in Winnipeg: data from the Winnipeg Street Census 2015.

Age matters?

Having a youth-centred and holistic approach to defining youth homelessness is essential simply because age matters. The causes of youth homelessness are distinct from adult homelessness, and the strategies employed to prevent and end youth homeless are also fundamentally different. Research suggests that youth most commonly experience what is called "hidden homelessness." This means that youth are precariously housed on friend's couches or staying with family members but knowing that they may be told to leave at any point.[8] They may be couch surfing, then have stable housing, then back to homelessness and at youth shelters within relatively short periods of time. Therefore, rigid categories or definitions of homelessness cannot be applied that might exclude young people who are struggling to find stable and predictable housing.

Structural, systemic, family and individual factors shape the pathways by which youth become homeless. Poverty and homelessness are influenced by the interaction between persons and their physical and social environments.[9] Since

84 per cent of homeless youth in Winnipeg identify as Indigenous, it is impossible to discuss and understand youth homelessness in Winnipeg without addressing the historical and contemporary processes and destructive legacy of colonization. Colonization refers to the complex set of discriminatory and oppressive practices that originated from the Western expansion into North America.[10]

Poverty certainly comprises a common pathway into youth homelessness, and Manitoba has the highest rate of child poverty in all of Canada.[11] Indigenous people in Winnipeg have almost double the poverty rate as the general population (17 per cent versus 10 per cent). Further, unemployment rates are almost three times higher. Youth growing up in families experiencing poverty and unemployment are also more likely to be connected to multiple government systems (e.g., child welfare, health, justice) that have great difficulty coordinating with each other. Homelessness often occurs as youth transition from or between these systems without the means, skills or supports needed for success.

According to the 2015 Winnipeg Street Census, 68.2 per cent of youth experiencing homelessness in Winnipeg spent time in the care of Child and Family Services.[12] Manitoba has one of the highest rates of children in State care: In 2017, there were 10,714 children in care, and the period 2006–2017 saw a 61.6 per cent increase of children in care. Of the total number of children in care of Child and Family Services, 9,535 (or 89 per cent) are Indigenous.[13] For the vast majority of youth, and particularly Indigenous youth, child welfare involvement is a profoundly negative experience. Many youth experience housing instability even while in care, including running away and placement breakdowns.

Family and individual factors leading to homelessness are intricately connected to structural and systemic factors.

The relationship between family conflict and youth homelessness is well documented.[14] Family conflict, breakdown or violence was the most frequently cited reason for individuals' first experience of homelessness in Winnipeg; this is consistent with findings across Canada and internationally.[15] However, youth homelessness is not merely the result of failure on the part of individual youth or their parents, but rather stems from a breakdown of the parent-child relationship. This breakdown often comes as the result of complex social factors such as economic stress, peer influences and community violence.

Indigenous homelessness

Indigenous youth homelessness is also distinct from generalized youth homelessness. Advocates and researchers have declared homelessness among Indigenous youth to be a rapidly growing national emergency. However, Indigenous youth are not a homogenous population. They comprise a group that encompasses a multitude of unique cultural backgrounds, legal status, experiences, strengths, skills and perspectives. Many are survivors of extreme poverty, racism, mental health issues in families and communities, disconnection from birth families, violence, sexual abuse and/ or neglect — all of which can be traced to the shared and continued history of colonialism. Indigenous youth have described experiencing not only physical homelessness but also spiritual homelessness, a "crisis of personal identity wherein a person's understanding or knowledge of how they relate to country, family and Aboriginal identity systems is confused or lacking."[16]

Indigenous homelessness is a "human condition that describes First Nations, Metis and Inuit, individuals, families or communities lacking stable, permanent, appropriate housing, or the immediate prospect, means or ability, to acquire such housing."[17] When viewed through a composite lens of Indigenous worldviews, it is very distinct from the common colonialist definition of homelessness. These include: individuals, families and communities isolated from their relationships to land, water, place, family, kin, each other, animals, cultures, languages and identities. Most importantly, Indigenous people experiencing these kinds of homelessness cannot culturally, spiritually, emotionally or physically reconnect with their Indigeneity or lost relationships.[18]

To understand Indigenous youth homelessness, therefore, it must been seen in the context of long-standing legacies and effects of colonization. Responses to youth homelessness must be rooted in an understanding that Indigenous peoples hold rights under the Canadian constitution, including the right to self-determination and self-government, and the right to practice one's own culture and customs, including language and religion.

Winnipeg's first youth homelessness strategy – Here and Now: Winnipeg's Plan to End Youth Homelessness

Youth experience homelessness differently than adults and thus, the strategies to end and prevent youth homelessness must also be distinct. There needed to be a tailored, youth-focused, culturally appropriate response that focused on the unique needs of youth.

In 2014, End Homelessness Winnipeg released *Winnipeg's Ten-Year Plan to End Homelessness*. Release of the plan prompted a group of youth-serving agencies to join forces and create a youth-specific strategy. Kelly Holmes, Executive Director of RaY and one of the authors of this chapter, contacted several local leaders who had been working to prevent, reduce and end youth homelessness to come together and guide the plan's direction. Together with generous support from the Winnipeg Foundation and the Government of Manitoba, confirmed in 2015, the vision of a shared strategy was realized.

The funding provided the resources needed to genuinely engage community stakeholders, in particular youth, in the planning process. The consultation process was extensive and was grounded in the voices of youth with experience of homelessness in Winnipeg, substantiated by the experience of practitioners and informed by research.

In October 2016, Here and Now: Winnipeg's Plan to End Youth Homelessness was launched. Holmes noted at the time that the plan called for "a more collaborative, integrated approach to youth homelessness" and that with the help of systems integration, professionals devoted to the problem hoped to "ensure that there are safety nets available to catch any youth that will fall."[19]

Youth-serving agencies in Winnipeg are shifting their response to youth homelessness

As with the rest of Canada, Winnipeg's historical response to youth homelessness was largely focused on reactive emergency and crisis response systems. While emergency responses are necessary, by definition they are not designed to address the broader problem of the very existence of youth homelessness. To radically reduce the number of homeless youth in Winnipeg, we must shift our collective response to focus on prevention and early intervention, and many youth-serving agencies in Winnipeg have been doing precisely that. As space here does not allow for a comprehensive review of this shift, we'll examine how two specific agencies, RaY and Ndinawe, are using an early intervention approach to implement planned, supported and healthy transitions for youth experiencing homelessness.

By an "early intervention perspective," RaY means it's in a hurry to create a meaningful relationship with a newly arrived young person and swiftly connect the person to the services that will be necessary to achieve personal objectives. Speed is of the essence. RaY knows it cannot wait for young people to find new paths to personal success without assistance.

In the simplest terms, RaY intervenes early, applying two steps. The first is to immediately protect the young person from coercion, the cold, hunger, thirst and medical danger. RaY deploys Homeless Outreach Mentors, who work in tandem with support workers to provide immediate, emergency housing services to youth participants. RaY begins to build a relationship with the young person by addressing these essential needs.

Once stabilized, the second step is immediately taken, which is all about the rapid connection to services. Programming at RaY is based on the social determinants of health with the understanding that shelter does not comprise the "end game." One of the social determinants, housing, figures prominently in this approach. RaY's housing department boasts a full continuum of housing support for youth. RaY offers young people access to any of the housing programs listed below based on a personalized case plan.

Housing First: The RaY Housing First program utilizes an Intensive Case Management philosophy to provide chronically or episodically homeless youth who face complex obstacles with access to stable, permanent housing. Staff roles range from finding initial housing placements for participants, forming and maintaining landlord partnerships, connecting youth to essential mental health and addictions services and providing peer support to goal planning and strategizing with youth to enable them to meet their goals.

Non-Housing First: The Non-Housing First team is multi-faceted, including a Basic Needs Coordinator, Cultural Program Manager and Housing Support Worker. The idea behind this program is that while youth often require assistance with housing, they also have needs beyond shelter, including cultural support and improved access to basic needs such as laundry, showers, clothing and toiletries.

RaY's Emergency Shelter and Transition Program (REST): The REST program is a transitional housing program that aims to stabilize youth and provide them with the life skills and resources they need to enter into healthy adulthood. The REST Case Coordinator works to house and support youth in fifteen units provided through a partnership with Manitoba Housing and located in Winnipeg's downtown core.

RaY's Optional Occupancy and Mentorship/Safe Suites Program (ROOM): ROOM is a three-year demonstration project developed through an innovative partnership between Child and Family Services, Manitoba Housing, and RaY. This is a prevention initiative to house youth that are transitioning from CFS care. The ROOM Team Lead and three case managers work with a small group of youth who require intensive case management.

RaY doesn't stop at housing. Social determinants are holistic in nature and encompass measures to address gaps in income, education, employment, social networks, housing and mental wellness. RaY works with young people on all of these social determinants at once, emphasizing those which the young person has expressed priority interest. RaY attempts to wrap supports around the young person with a view to building a sustainable exit path from homelessness.

Ndinawemaaganag Endaawaad Inc. (Ndinawe) is a Winnipeg-based youth agency that, like RaY, has also shifted its response to youth homelessness. It is an integrated service organization for youth, focusing on shelter, culture, recreation, education, outreach and support since 1993.

Ndinawe, which translates to "our relatives' home," is an Indigenous, community-based organization that has offered a variety of programs and resources aimed at improving the social, cultural and economic outcomes for young people in Winnipeg for twenty-five years. To achieve its mission, Ndinawe provides for a strong continuum of integrated programs and supportive services.

This service array can be grouped into a number of categories. The first is upstream in the prevention area. Ndinawe is proud to be able to serve a clientele that extends outside the strict limits of the shelter, namely young people who are not homeless but are at risk thereof. Ndinawe works in close partnership with community agencies to both identify and support these individuals. Prevention is not the usual business of a youth homeless shelter, but Ndinawe has found that the best way to reduce homelessness is to actually prevent it in the first place. The organization's efforts to prevent youth homelessness in Winnipeg include:

The Outreach Team: This team works with other agencies to provide outreach services, including harm-reduction supports for various high-risk activities in the community. The team provides no-barrier access to resources such as harm-reduction kits that include condoms, lubrication and information about relevant services; it also offers services such as crisis interventions, transportation and harm-reduction based addiction interventions.

Outreach Workers: Outreach Workers connect with and provide support to vulnerable youth in the community who may be at risk for or experiencing sexual exploitation. They employ daily foot patrols in the community and nightly vehicle patrols.

The Ndinawe Youth Transitional School: This facility offers a structured and integrated learning environment for youth in transition from formal school. In partnership with RB Russell, the transitional school provides a positive educational atmosphere for youth in transition.

Ndinawe Youth Resource Centre: This is a 24/7 Indigenous youth drop-in centre that provides youth aged thirteen to twenty-four a safe space as an alternative to the streets by engaging them in a wide variety of programs and resources, including:

- Drop-in space for youth to connect, develop positive relationships within their community, engage in a variety of activities and have access to computers, television, movies, video games, ping pong, board games and outings.
- The North End Arts Centre provides high quality arts and cultural programming to youth to engage and empower them though creative expression, self-discovery and skill-building.
- The Sports and Recreational program engages youth in healthy physical activities.
- The Cooking Program ensures youth have nutritious meals each night and engages youth in learning basic life skills.

The Ndinawe Youth Resource Centre remains open twenty-four hours a day to ensure youth have immediate, barrier-free access to a place of safety in times of crisis when other resources may not be available to them.

The Wahkotowin Strengthening Families program: This is a fourteen-week curriculum-based program that engages youth between the ages of eleven and seventeen, along with their families who are facing system challenges and barriers, such as access to education and employment.

Youth Care Worker Certificate Program: A community-based academic program offered in partnership with Red River College that provides accredited training to obtain a Child and Youth Care certificate.

Wahkohtowin: A fourteen-week skill development program for families of youth eleven to seventeen years of age that seeks to strengthen bonds, increase communication and decrease conflict among family members.

Ndinawe also provides emergency response for young people who are homeless. Like RaY, Ndinawe's emergency services are designed to stabilize young people and make them safe as a first step to starting the hard work of finding a permanent avenue off the streets. To this end, the Ndinawemaaganag Endaawaad Safe House provides a safe and nurturing home for male, female and transgender youth ages eleven to seventeen who are in need of emergency shelter and who are otherwise vulnerable and at risk of experiencing serious physical, emotional or spiritual harm. The youth safe house is a sixteen-bed facility that provides accessible twenty-four-hour shelter and necessities for Winnipeg children and youth who are living on the streets, are at risk of abuse and exploitation or in need of a safe place to stay. In an average year, approximately 5,500 nights of food, shelter and support were provided to children and youth in the community.

Once stabilized, Ndinawe offers a suite of programs, including housing, to young people to prepare for the journey out of homelessness. At the youth resource centre, youth are able to access employment and housing resources upon arrival as well as schedule a variety of programming, special events and counseling supports and resources. These are overviews of other community programs available in Winnipeg:

Chu Manitou Tanka Oyati Tipi: An innovative transitional living program that offers stable, supportive housing for youth who are significantly at higher risk for more negative outcomes than their peers due to multiple, chronic risk factors, including chronic involvement with the child welfare system, street involvement and sexual exploitation.

650 Burrows Location: This location will house specialized programming focused on addressing the unique challenges of youth aged eighteen to twenty-four who are chronically homeless.

RaY and Ndinawe are both shifting from a primarily emergency response to youth homelessness to a multi-pronged approach to prevention and early intervention as described above. Their programs also focus on healing from trauma and reconnecting with culture, which is important for Indigenous youth. The future of shelters for youth is no-barrier access to a safe space that implements a supported and healthy transition for youth experiencing homelessness. Youth are connected to resources and supports for housing, employment, education, wellness and healing. Youth safe spaces create a safety net for youth and opportunities for gaining the skills, resources and supports necessary to successfully transition, maintain housing and thrive.

The place is here and the time is now

Winnipeg's Plan to End Youth Homelessness is an ambitious plan, and it is Winnipeg's first youth-specific strategy to end and prevent youth homelessness. It represents a call to action. Everyone plays a role in ending and preventing youth homelessness. The role of the shelters in Winnipeg is clear: prevent youth homelessness where possible and, where it proves impossible, intervene quickly to stabilize young people and get them on the road to a better place. The shelter and the street are no place for young people. Every extra day spent without stable housing increases the risks of a whole range of very bad things happening to youth. We have the moral responsibility to do better. However, shelters can only do so much by themselves. Winnipeg's plan makes clear we're all in this together. It is the young who will pay the price if we don't each pull our weight.

"We need a plan because we need to be safe. We can make the streets safer for the youth that are on the streets, reduce suicide, and get youth off the streets if we work together with this plan."

— Savannah, Youth

CHAPTER 8
The Community Hub

Cora Gajari, Regina, SK

Perspective

I am the Executive Director at Carmichael Outreach Inc. in Regina, Saskatchewan, a small community-based organization that has been in existence for thirty years. We work to respond to the needs of people experiencing homelessness or at risk of experiencing homelessness. Most of the people we work with have experienced intergenerational poverty, have inherited the trauma of colonialism and the residential school system and live with physical and mental health issues and addictions. Our three main pillars of service involve a meal service, free boutique that provides clothing and household items and housing support.

Most of the people we serve struggle with and within paternalistic systems such as child protection, health care and criminal justice, and we do our best to actively and aggressively advocate on their behalf. Because of the need for organizational autonomy to advocate effectively for the men and women we serve, we try as much as possible to avoid government funding and to rely largely on event fundraising and donations from the community, community groups, churches and corporations. This autonomy attracted me to Carmichael Outreach Inc., along with the fact that the organization is pretty much ground zero for people who struggle in our community, turns almost no one away and provides as many needed barrier-free services as possible.

I got into this work because of what I call my "advocate spirit." I think I was born with it, and then it was further ingrained in me through life experience. Some of these experiences were brutal, violent and scarring. Coming to terms with these lessons and learning to live with the scars led me to my current path. I am proud of my path, and I don't regret any of the trauma I have experienced. My past as an Indigenous interracially adopted female child and my experiences of sexual/physical/domestic violence have made me familiar with the challenges faced by others. My experience with racism and its impact on me forced me to deconstruct not only racism as a social phenomenon but also my own identity to confront my demons, including mental health issues and addictions as a result of my abuse — all of which meant I had to put many fractured pieces back together again, imperfectly, but stronger than ever.

I have learned that people are not their labels. People are far more multi-dimensional than "homeless," an "alcoholic" or an "addict." Being labelled myself has helped me to understand that one either lives by the labels or beyond/ despite them. Once confronted with the existence of labels, it is ultimately one's own choice how to relate to them. Living past the labels has helped me become a considerably more resilient and empathetic person than I otherwise would have been.

We most often can't even understand our own acceptance or use of stereotypes because the labels we use to construct them are inherited from pre-existing ideas and are learned unconsciously and unquestioningly. Everyone uses these labels in order to define social situations and their place within them. These labels, however, are subject to imperfection at best and erroneous stigma and discrimination at worst.

When people in positions of power, who are disproportionately socioeconomically privileged, incorporate these labels/understandings/concepts into policies and laws, they become entrenched in our structures, institutions and processes. They become very difficult to change — particularly because they are rooted in the unconscious identity of the privileged. Because I have been labelled, resulting powerlessness and privilege at different times, I can see these labels quite clearly. I feel it is my responsibility to not only challenge these labels, but to see people for whom they are beyond these labels. In my opinion, the ability to do so is a privilege since I haven't met a lot of unlikeable or unreachable people in my life.

The shelter of tomorrow will have to do better in addressing the way power, racism and stereotyping affects homeless people suffering from deep and damaging trauma. The future of the homeless shelter in my view is as a Community Hub which, first and foremost, is equipped to quickly earn the respect and trust of individuals who have been spurned by more formal systems of care (like hospitals, addiction centres, social services, welfare offices and the criminal justice system). As a Community Hub, the shelter can serve as both a safe and reliable access point and an advocate for homeless people to connect to the services and supports that are necessary to propel them into healthy and sustainable housing and communities. It should also directly offer services that equip homeless people to make quick and permanent exits from homelessness. Homeless people present at the shelter, often in desperation, because they have not been able to obtain essential supports from government agencies. As Community Hubs with deep expertise in social systems, wide knowledge of available government services and an array of carefully crafted exit programs of their own, I hope that all shelters will one day have the capacity to walk alongside these often complex individuals the next time they knock on those State agency doors.

People of the shelter

A Community Hub will sometimes be successful in stabilizing homeless people and accompanying them to a better place, and sometimes it won't. However, the likelihood of success rises as the shelter improves its ability to deliver the core competencies of a Community Hub — namely earning trust, preparing options for a permanent exit from homelessness and advocating forcefully for services and supports for departing clients.

Debbie sits hunched, almost protectively, scribbling away with pen and paper in the almost empty coffee room. She works patiently, sometimes for hours. I rarely see her actually drinking coffee. These days her drink is water in her ever-present Pepsi bottle. I have seen her drink alcohol. It used to be every day to mass excess, both beverage and non-beverage alcohol (e.g., mouth wash and hand sanitizer). She calls me little sister and has adopted my children as her own (and threatened my husband if he wasn't good to me!).

Debbie can be manipulative, even with me. She puts on an act, but I don't usually call her on it, because I accept that this is a well-rehearsed survival skill and her existence despite the odds is proof that is has worked. So, who am I to call her on it? Tired and drained one time, I was sitting in the coffee room and she told me about her life in residential school. During a field trip, she had fallen into a river and was carried downstream by a strong current. I know the river of which she was speaking, and it is an obvious analogy for her own journey. She survived the river and residential school and the streets.

She asks me to make copies of her artwork and poetry. I know how she likes it done — four copies, and I get to keep the originals. Once in a while, I carry the originals with me to read as inspiration. I have known Debbie for almost five years. Two years after we helped her find transitional housing and provided her with supports, she secured a permanent home of her own in the very place where she had succeeded in quitting drinking. With our support, she was finally able to create some stability for herself.

Frank had curly grey hair. He was a big, smiling, friendly man, polite to a fault. I am pretty sure he had a crush on one of the women working in the kitchen. He came for coffee almost every day. Greeting everyone kindly, he would stick his head into the kitchen to make sure all was okay and to share a laugh with the women. Sometimes, stopping at the boutique, he would take a look around to see what clothes or trinkets were we had. He made his coffee, then sat down to talk and laugh with everyone around him. On his way out, he would pick up takeaway lunches, always two, and bid us goodbye.

Our old building was cold, and although I am proud of my Inuvialuit ancestry, I do believe I would have died from the cold in the land of my ancestors! Walking to the kitchen to warm up one day, I jumped slightly as I felt a weight land on my shoulders. I turned to see Frank putting a multi-coloured jacket on me to keep me warm. He smiled at me with his whole face — I know it sounds cliché, but Frank's eyes actually *did* twinkle when he smiled!

He had been evicted from his low rental housing unit for what was essentially a mental health issue, the main symptom being hoarding. I had heard he was sleeping rough in Victoria Park. In the winter of 2018, I was having dinner with my husband and son in a local pub on a very cold and snowy day when I received the message that Frank was gone. These deaths are always sudden and shocking, and a million thoughts go through our minds at Carmichael. Did he pass away outside in the elements? It wouldn't have been in detox because he didn't drink. It wasn't in a shelter because they were all full. I felt a little more at peace to find out later that Frank had passed away suddenly in the kitchen at his friend's house where he had stopped by to shower. Not alone and with a friend, he had some measure of dignity and support at the end. Everyone blamed the intolerance of the housing corporation and the staff's unwillingness to work with Frank through what was obviously a well-known mental health problem. What is that called again . . . tenant relations?

Months later at a book launch at Carmichael, my Mom said to me, "that jacket made it full circle, didn't it?" (i.e., the multi-coloured jacket Frank had given to me to keep me warm). It turns out that my own mother had donated it to our boutique. A chill, a happy one, ran down the back of my neck to my fingertips. I then told my Mom all about Frank and showed her his picture on our memorial wall. There is one in the kitchen also. We will not forget him anytime soon.

Dennis slept outside or in detox. For fourteen years. Three times he was accidentally transported in a garbage truck and hauled outside city limits to the dump, having spent the night in a dumpster. He was a regular at Carmichael Outreach long before we worked with him on housing. We helped him find a place of his own and set up a space with all of his favourite things, including a television, DVD, VHS players and a lot of music. We also got him a kitten. On our Managed Alcohol Program (MAP), he has nine beers per day and has stabilized significantly. He now has two part-time jobs, which give him a purpose. His fellow co-workers can now see a bit through the labels. They bought him a cake to celebrate his one-year anniversary of employment at the tire shop.

On the weekends, Dennis would fall back into his old habits of drinking non-beverage alcohol. While consuming or recovering from consuming, his behaviour would become erratic, teary one moment and raging the next. His house was being taken over by friends and acquaintances that still lived the same lifestyle he had for those fourteen years. Because he couldn't let himself be considered a rat and couldn't say "no" to them, he felt helpless to keep them out of his place.

We worked to provide weekend supports for Dennis, but what he really needed was secure, twenty-four-hour supported care that facilitated a MAP. Such an arrangement was impossible to put in place for Dennis. Accommodation adapted to his needs, though technically possible, was never achievable, either because he was not eligible financially or the landlords simply don't want a formerly homeless and actively using First Nations addict in their homecare environment and they find a way to deny him a place. The discrimination is based on income, race and health condition — labelling at its worst. It's illegal but too hard to fight. Ironically, after a long process, we found out that a medical assessment from twenty years ago recommended supported living in a group home.

The housing challenges faced by all these members of the Carmichael family are exacerbated by health problems. Most of the people coming through our doors forego regular preventative health care, and many suffer from chronic medical conditions that go untreated. Debbie suffers from ovarian cancer that she chooses not to treat. Refusing treatment for cancer and other chronic health issues such as HIV and Hepatitis C is common in this population. As an Indigenous person, despite being educated and gainfully employed, I have personally experienced the humiliation of racial discrimination in our health care system on numerous occasions. I can only imagine how some of my Carmichael family must feel. I am not completely surprised they opt to risk their lives to avoid yet one more humiliating and disempowering experience at the hands of professionals.

Debbie and Dennis suffer from addiction. Like racialized people, addicts are often the victims of discrimination as well. Mainstream Alcoholic Anonymous and Narcotics Anonymous meetings are supposed to be open to people of all walks of life, but actually, addicts experiencing extreme poverty and homelessness are regularly frowned upon and degraded in these meetings.

Add mental illness to the equation. For Carmichael clients, mental health problems are prevalent and generally arise from incidences of life trauma, which include deeply personal experiences of having been sexually abused or the degrading abuses that happened in their families, residential schools or foster care. The lack of trust commonly held by our folks prevents them from accessing mainstream mental health care, often leaving them to treat themselves with intoxicating substances.

The Community Hub model I propose below to guide the future development of shelters must have not only the capacity to successfully connect its clients to housing and health services, it must even more importantly have the ability to earn the trust of individuals who are deeply distrustful regarding our traditional medical structures of care.

The shelter

Homeless shelters exist because they serve a purpose, both for people experiencing homelessness and for those whose job it is to address homelessness. People experiencing homelessness go to shelters for help; people who create shelters do so in an attempt to alleviate (or one could argue to hide) homelessness, temporarily, while offering a person shelter. People who use the shelters are significantly different than the people who create the shelters and have very little say in how shelters are run and what they could and should do.

Shelters are extremely expensive, and the research shows it often costs more to keep people in shelters than it does to house them, even with supports. In Regina, as in many other cities, shelters are filled to capacity and sometimes over-capacity; and communities and governments have scrambled to develop emergency measures to address the lack of shelter space. As an example of extreme scrambling, in winter 2015, a gentleman in his eighties came to Carmichael to use our shower program. He used a walker and moved with significant difficulty. After calling paramedics because he fell in the shower, we discovered he had a history of falls and obviously was struggling with serious health issues related to his balance and mobility. All the shelters in the city were full, including ours, so he was taken to city police cells for the weekend for his own safety. I often wonder how he felt that weekend, to be extremely vulnerable, sick, have nowhere to go — and then be treated like a criminal.

To be fair, I would argue that most people who work in this area do not see shelters as a way to stack and hide people experiencing homelessness; however, the powers that be — often the funders, policy-makers and other decision-makers with the power to shape shelters — are working from an outdated and simplistic idea of homelessness. They believe that *people experience homelessness because they are poor*. Poverty is to blame, and the remedy is to impose upon the individuals experiencing it the responsibility of extracting themselves from that state of poverty.

Society has traditionally categorized two types of poor — the "deserving poor" and the "undeserving poor." The widow and the orphan represent two typical examples of the former. According to this worldview, the deserving poor are poor due to circumstances not of their choosing. The "undeserving poor," by contrast, are believed to be poor because of their own bad choices. Their poverty results from a lack of motivation, poor coping skills or laziness. There is little public sympathy for this group and they don't deserve the same supports since they are the authors of their own destruction and despair. Homeless people are treated like undeserving poor people and are marginalized as a result.

For the most part, shelters have been designed around the notion that clients come from the ranks of the undeserving poor, and this notion continues to shape policies and services. For example, men's shelters commonly take men in at night and turn them out in the morning for the day only to take them back in at day's end so that they can eat, shower and sleep. The understanding is that the men should spend their day looking for work to end their homelessness.

This is a profoundly simplistic expectation. Chronically homeless people cannot be expected to find their way to housing, health and employment alone. They are homeless in part because they could not do so. In my experience at Carmichael Outreach Inc., many of the people who are experiencing homelessness, addictions, mental health issues and chronic poverty were employed or getting their education at some point in their lives; none of them planned this path for themselves growing up.

The reality

The reality is that poverty and homelessness have complex causes. Still in the common imagination, because it is more visible, poverty is understood to be the cause of mental health problems, addictions, homelessness, criminal justice involvement and a host of other social ills. My main argument, always, is that poverty — like addictions, mental illness and homelessness — is a symptom of something else, usually trauma.

Jason is chronically addicted, has no permanent residence and from time to time expresses suicidal thoughts to me in my office. He told me how he traces it back to grade five when he was sexually assaulted in residential school. He said he became numb and foggy, couldn't concentrate on school and would sit through the day blankly. The first time he used drugs, his pain was alleviated, and he couldn't stop. Now addicted and living on the streets, he struggles to stay on methadone or medical marijuana. It is clear to me that finding employment will not provide a remedy for his trauma, addictions or homelessness.

I often think of the resilience of the people who use our services, especially when I hear bits and pieces of their stories. Having had similar experiences, although not nearly to the same degree, I can relate to the obstacles they face. I have been asked to speak as a role model and example for others because of my Indigenous heritage, having been a teenaged Mom, having experienced domestic violence and having stayed in shelters to escape it. I agree on one condition — that it be understood my experience is not the same as anyone else's. Growing up, I inherited a lot of benefits. My parents both have post-secondary education, encouraged me to be conscientious and an academic. I had support when times were tough, including financial support. My parents read to me, and growing up, I experienced privilege (which ironically made it harder when I experienced discrimination later in life). I explain that all of this was inherited and not the product of my hard work. The people I am often asked to be a role model for need to understand I had the benefit of assets and privileges they may not have. It is like comparing apples to oranges. In their resilience to the kind of profound challenges I may not have faced as a child, I see their innovative strength and unbelievable survival skills in a world where the odds are stacked against them from the get-go. I see in them the power of our humanity and the potential to survive despite the odds.

Community Hubs

To a large extent, shelters function to hide homelessness and were never intended to do much more than that. As such they can actually perpetuate the problem by keeping it out of the public eye and forcing homeless people into a day-to-day survivalist mode. However, as I alluded to earlier, because shelters are where most visibly homeless people are, they are in a prime position to shift to a "Community Hub model" that can genuinely help people rebuild the foundations for change in their lives.

The temporary or emergency nature of many shelters is not conducive to a welcoming and homelike environment in which trusting relationships are fostered. At Carmichael Outreach, we work to create an inclusive environment that is more like a family community than an institutional centre providing professional services. In this environment we can establish relationships built on trust and mutual respect, and we have been able to establish connections with people who are otherwise unreachable, due to various traumatic life experiences.

The Community Hub at Carmichael Outreach Inc. in Regina

Through these relationships a person's deeper issues become apparent. Until then, one can only base assumptions about what a person may need on observations. Going back to the individuals described earlier in this chapter, all of them needed help, and for the most part, this is true of the vast majority if not all people experiencing or at risk of experiencing homelessness.

Shelters built on a Community Hub model will hire and train staff to be deeply sensitive to the troubled paths clients have journeyed, listeners of the humblest kind and profoundly patient in discovering opportunities to help these individuals onto better and more healthy trajectories. This is the first of three key capacities of Community Hub shelters.

The Community Hub model would bring medical, psychological and spiritual services directly to the people who need them in an environment that fosters trust and healing. Shelters operating on this model are profoundly different from existing centres or agencies because of this emphasis on the relationship of caring and respect. Needs assessment, case management and professional support are of course also present, but only in the context of a trauma-informed practice.

Transitional housing during the process of assessing and addressing needs provides temporary stability for a person working on their growth. Besides medical and mental health services, practical programming could be available to assist people with their transition to being independently housed. Life skills classes with material geared to the needs of partici-pants could be one such program; this is always requested of Carmichael Outreach.

Many people who have suffered trauma find solace in exploring their spiritual needs. A disproportionate number of people who are homeless or at risk are Indigenous and have experienced separation from their culture, family and communities. Requests for an Elder, smudging and cere-mony are frequent, particularly for those who have been through the residential school and foster care systems. The new shelter could provide a safe space for people to explore their spiritual connectedness; this has frequently been cited as a best practice by those who have recovered from addictions and from living on the streets, whether through Christianity or traditional Indigenous culture.

This set of capacities, from housing expertise, psychologi-cal support, life skills and spiritual and cultural exploration, represent the second part of the Community Hub model.

The third and final one has at its roots the imbalance of power between homeless people and institutional actors. In a nutshell, shelter people cannot get the kind of state support they need without a strong advocate in their corner. Fighting institutional discrimination and exclusion is tough enough for someone without the baggage of trauma and illness. With this baggage, it's virtually impossible to access the benefits and services, including health, justice and financial supports that are due to and required by them to survive and thrive.

Shelters organized on the Community Hub model will be that advocate and will lobby and fight with increasing success if they have the trust of their clientele and the content expertise to cut through bureaucratic red tape. As a person who has tried to access services for trauma, the search is daunting with professionals who are unable to relate to or address trauma related to violence or sexual assaults in the "language" that is needed by the people seeking the services. The majority of professionals in this field live worlds away from our Carmichael family and are at a loss as to how to help or cannot provide help that is effective. When we have had to access services for clients, the experience has been very disheartening, frustrating and at times, disgusting. Our folks have been treated very poorly by a system of "professionals" who do not understand them, hold various degrees of disgust and resentment toward them, which easily translates in various degrees of intolerance, disdain and abuse. This is why advocacy skills are necessary in the shelters of the future.

Conclusion

The concepts that have shaped homeless shelters are not only outdated, they are false. Not only are they outdated and false, they result in the perpetual victimization of people who have experienced trauma and end up in poverty, struggling with addictions, mental health issues and homelessness. Reshaping shelters in recognition of the humanity of people experiencing homelessness and an understanding of the supports that they need would alleviate homelessness significantly. Homeless shelters can evolve purposefully to become profoundly trauma-informed and sensitive in their approach, skilled in the priority areas that matter to homeless people, especially in housing and health care, offer preparatory programs to exit homelessness and relentlessly battle existing power structures to make services available to homeless people, thus ensuring they will no longer need them. Shelters as Community Hubs can address homelessness more effectively than most shelters as currently constructed. I think it's the way forward to reduce homelessness in Canada.

CHAPTER 9
A New Model of Care

Dr. John Rook, Calgary, AB

It has been an honour to work in the homeless-serving sector for much of my career. In that time, I have been privileged to meet some incredible, resilient, and interesting people. My experience has taught me that no two people are exactly alike. I have learned that each person's journey to homelessness is unique, and using a "one size fits all" approach to helping people out of it is ineffective.

I walked into my first homeless shelter as an eighteen-year-old volunteer. I quickly noticed that it was a place focused on survival. The shelter was a place to seek refuge from the cold and to get a warm meal. There was no effort to empower clients to move out and up in the world. The first homeless person with whom I had a conversation told me that he had been "saved" (in the Christian sense) in twenty-three different shelters and that was how you got the best services — going to the chapel and confessing your sins got you first spot in the food line. I knew at age eighteen that something was wrong with this picture.

Years later, I talked with my fellow shelter workers about limited resources, resolving conflicts between clients, handing out hygiene items and bus tickets and rationing food. The societal thinking that these people needed fixing was prevalent. People in the shelter were treated as though they were somehow flawed human beings in need of correction. I always knew that socks, a mat on the floor and a meal — as necessary as they might be when you are destitute — were not the solution to homelessness.

Throughout my career, I have been pleased to witness a drastic change in the homeless shelter as an institution. There has been a shift in thinking away from simply providing people with basic necessities. We have begun to understand that a hand-up is more effective than a handout. We have begun to understand that offering integrated services in addition to emergency shelter is crucial to help clients exit homelessness. This model, which I will discuss below, took a long time to develop. There has been a shift from seeing people as broken to seeing the system as broken. As we have moved to a coordinated system of care, we have seen significant numbers move from homeless to housed, from unhealthy to wellness. This is a truly new model of care for homeless people and potentially a template for other shelters across the country.

While this chapter is about best practices in homeless sheltering, I want to say that of equal or even greater importance is homelessness prevention. This is rarely addressed in conversations about homelessness, but I believe it is critical to do so. People are tumbling fast over the chaotic waterfall of life into the swirling waters below. We have done an admirable job of providing life boats (shelters) to rescue people from the tumult. What we have not done is go upstream to see why they are falling into the river in the first place. It is not too early to begin thinking not only about care and cure, but also about prevention. If society puts its efforts there, then we can stop the flow into homelessness.

As I think about the future of the homeless shelter, I am encouraged and hopeful that the progress we have made will continue. What follows will shed some light on the direction I hope the shelter sector is heading in.

Why are people homeless?

No one questions the fact that people are homeless in Canada. How many are homeless is difficult to answer, as hidden homelessness is impossible to measure; the Homeless Hub (www.homelesshub.ca) estimates that as many as 50,000 people comprise the "hidden homeless." While we use the term "couch surfing" for these people, many are not even on a couch in someone's home. People who don't want to be found are hidden everywhere. I have talked with people in Winnipeg in –30 degree Celsius weather who were living behind a four by eight foot sheet of plywood leaning against a building. I once knew a man who lived in a small cave that he dug into the side bank of the Bow River in Calgary. He didn't die in the 2013 Calgary flood, but his "home" was destroyed. His hidden life helps explain why the numbers of hidden homeless people are so difficult to determine.

The only numbers that can be used with confidence come from the counts made by Canada's homeless shelters, domestic violence shelters and temporary institutions. As we consider why people are homeless, it is worth also considering the prison population — where homeless people are incarcerated for survival crimes and drug crime. While in prison, one could argue that they are only temporarily housed as they will be released to homelessness when their sentence is served. Unless such an individual has gone through a drug treatment court for their crime, it is highly unlikely that they will have a prison exit plan other than going back onto the street or into a homeless shelter.

The question then of why people are homeless is complex. My observations from many years in the shelter field and hundreds of conversations with shelter guests suggest that trauma is a significant factor. Childhood abuse, brain injury, domestic violence, inability to obtain employment because of how a person looks or other stigmatizing characteristics make up just some of the causes. Society can be extremely mean to people who don't fit our stereotype of what a person should be or look like. I will return to this presently.

Some factors that suggest themselves as causes of homelessness are more likely symptoms. Is poor health a cause or a symptom? Or both? What about addictions? Mental health issues? Lack of family and family supports? And then there is the issue of the criminalization of poverty.[1] In many places the treatment of poor people leads to incarceration. There are laws that prohibit panhandling and begging, which lead to fines that are impossible to pay, which leads to incarceration. Incarceration, in turn, leads to difficulty finding employment following release, which leads to an inability to find housing, which causes a person to reoffend to live, which leads to another incarceration. For many caught in the trap of homelessness, this vicious cycle offers no escape other than death. As J. Riemen said in 2013, "The rich get richer . . . and the poor get prison."

What we do know is that every person has a story. I believe stories must be unpacked if there is to be a chance of moving on. Life pain can make some people withdraw while others become angry. Unless we can understand someone's life pain, we are only responding to behaviours; this never solves the underlying issues and in fact only exacerbates them. We judge and incarcerate based on a behaviour or action instead of understanding the "why" of the action.

Some people say that there is no future in the past. As I think about the life pain of people in extreme poverty and homelessness, I disagree. Well-being is only possible when the past is confronted. I have watched people deal with their pain, reframe their story and move on successfully. I realize this is a lot to ask of shelter staff, so in what follows I'll suggest some solutions.

Is housing the (only) solution?

I believe that the problems shelters have created are actually bigger than the ones they were trying to solve. We have created many shelters where entrenchment into a chronic user mentality now seems almost unsolvable. Whether we want to admit it or not, some shelters for chronic users have become home. Clients and shelter staff have become family. Many shelters have become warehouses for seniors and chronic drug and alcohol users. People often say that they don't feel safe in shelters. Shelters are often understaffed by people who are underpaid and underqualified. Alcohol, drugs, theft and violence have become normal. Shelter staff often use a punitive approach simply because they are overwhelmed and are unable to manage the clientele. It is easier to suspend someone and ban them from the shelter than it is to work with the person to discover why they are homeless and what form a path to wellness and housing might take.

Without addressing it in detail, I would like to shine a light on the cost of keeping someone homeless, beginning with this key fact: it is more expensive to keep a person in a shelter in my city than it is to house that individual. The shelter for which I am responsible receives approximately $13,500 per bed annually, which does not include our food budget. We house people in our apartments at a cost of approximately $8,500 annually. In Calgary, the last homeless point-in-time count still notes that 3,200 people are homeless. The city estimates that the annual cost per homeless person is $55,000, while the cost to house a homeless person through Housing First is $21,000.

We know that homelessness isn't only about housing but it's always about housing. Using a Housing First model, people who are housed have access to better services and move forward better than those who are shelter housed. The stability of having your own place supports mental and physical wellness and healthy nutrition. When people are housed, we often see a significant drop in drug use.

Over sixty years ago, the federal government adopted the *National Housing Act* of 1954, thus making housing a government responsibility. Notwithstanding this responsibility, we are presently in a housing/homeless crisis in Canada. All orders of governments have set targets for ending homelessness, not-for-profit agencies and some faith groups have built low-income housing and even some developers have stepped up to assist.[2]

Housing offers only a partial solution; unless underlying issues are addressed, people will not be able to maintain their housing. We have found that loneliness is a significant factor in people losing their housing. People either violate their lease by allowing their friends to stay or they become so lonely that the streets or the shelter present a better option. In one of the programs I used to run, we had a client throw a television off his sixth-floor balcony. He was in a scattered-site apartment owned by a large low-income housing provider. The landlord wanted him evicted. I went to the apartment with a staff member to speak with the client. The staff member was very caring and asked him why he had done this. We were shocked by his answer when he said, "You came." His loneliness was so severe that even negative contact with people was better than no contact.

Just to finish that story, the landlord wanted to move him to the first floor, so he couldn't throw something else off the balcony and seriously injure or kill someone. The worker decided that since loneliness was the issue, he would work with him to build a network of good friends. The client is now in a bowling league and has found several people that he knows who live nearby. They get together regularly and attend one of the mental health organizations that provides day programming. He has even taken a trip with friends to Las Vegas! He still lives on the sixth floor.

Where do we go from here?

While it is true that many shelters are moving away from a warehousing model, there is still much to do. Many shelters in the past believed that their goal was to make people who were experiencing homelessness as comfortable as possible. To this end they provided a bed, meals, showers, laundry facilities, lockers and a few caring staff that often included a chaplain. Now, the model has shifted. Staff view themselves not as security but as "exit strategists" or "housing workers." Their job is not simply to make people comfortable but to assist them on their journey to wellness. A bed, a shower, a good meal and some free food does not end homelessness; in fact, these services may encourage entrenchment.

Recently, one of our shelter managers in Calgary asked shelter users two simple questions: how long have you been here, and what do you need from us? No one was asked why they needed a shelter in the first place or where they had been before entering the shelter. There were no demographics taken and intake forms were not reviewed. They were simply asked those two questions. This was not a scientific study; it was simply the questions of a manager who wanted to know how he could support people on their journey to wellness. Here's what he discovered . . .

There were two very distinct groupings, based on how long people had been in the shelter — specifically whether it had been less than a month or more than a month. Those who had been there less than a month said things like, "I need a place to live. I really need a job. It would be great to go back to school." Some said, "I need to get identification. Can you help me with my alimony? I miss my kids so much. Can you help me track them down?"

Those who had been there for more than a month said things like, "How do we change the channel on the TVs? Can you put in bigger ones? Why don't you let us have seconds on meals? Can you add time to the showers? These mats on the floor are awful. Can you put in real beds?"

The first group is teetering on the brink and could fall either way. The second group has fallen into the homeless void of entrenchment and entitlement. This confirmed what we believed — that shelter services themselves are part of the problem for many.

Beyond housing

I believe that shelter reform will be incomplete if we only address the current housing crisis. No one wants to be homeless and almost every one of the people I talk with in shelter and on the streets would love to have a place to call home. Perhaps more importantly, we must develop all the supporting interventions to keep people housed: proper identification, health care, dental care, mental

health counselors, addictions support, healthy relationships, adequate income through either employment or
government assistance and opportunities for educational
upgrades — these can move people forward.

I also believe that shelter reform will not be successful if
society doesn't change. Stigma is alive and well in Canada.
Indigenous people, recent immigrants and members of
the LGBTQ2S+ community feel significant discrimination because of how they look or speak. Despite significant
headway, racism, sexism and lots of other -isms are still very
much present in our world. It takes only a few moments on a
social media site to see bigotry, racism and a lack of care and
understanding for people who are viewed as different. These
are the people who have been ostracized from society and
now need the caring services of our shelter system.

Where I work in Calgary for the Mustard Seed Society,
we have a 370-bed homeless shelter. Ten years ago, the
shelter was set up for six months as a Winter Response
to our homeless crisis; now it is a permanent fixture. Our
$4,709,000 budget does not include food but does include
buses that transport our guests twelve kilometres from our
downtown buildings to what is now known as the Foothills
Shelter. It is a city-owned building in the Foothills industrial area of South East Calgary. Buses leave from our
downtown location at 5:30 and 6:30 p.m., arriving in time
for a 7:00 dinner. Buses leave the shelter in the morning
starting at 5:30 until 9:30 so people can get to work or to
services downtown.

The shelter itself has offices, a full-service kitchen,
dining room, locker room, amenities room, clothing room,
computer room and mats on the floor. There are fifty mats
for women and 320 for men. In the centre of the shelter is
"the bridge," which has glass all around so that staff can see

The Mustard Seed clothing room helps homeless people onto better paths.

and monitor every mat. Staff do regular "wellness rounds" all night long, and there are very few problems.

When you enter the shelter, there are two levels of intake. After the first level, you may be subjected to a random search. We believe that for the shelter to remain safe it is imperative that alcohol, drugs and weapons cannot be permitted. We confiscate drugs and weapons, but only if you chose to proceed to the second-level intake. Should you choose not to proceed, you are free to leave. Our position in both our shelter and our housing is that whatever is legal/illegal in the community is also legal/illegal in our buildings.

After you pass through security, there are several staff offices you must walk by to enter the dining room and sleeping area. These deal with housing, employment, chaplaincy and advocacy. This was intentional so that when staff in the shelter talk with guests they can remind them of the offices they passed as they entered the shelter. We believe you have rights, but rights are meaningless without responsibility. You have the right to the shelter. You have the responsibility to find a positive exit.

Our shelter workers do so much more than keep guests safe. Language matters. If you want something and if you can name it correctly, it is more likely to become a reality. With that in mind, we refer to the staff as "Exit Strategists," and their job is to engage with guests to help them find the supports they need to move forward. We have built a very relational shelter where everyone's name is important, everyone's story is important and helping our clients exit is what drives us. On the night shift when there is a lull and staff have time, they research housing options, which they can present to guests in the morning. This supports the work of the housing team. Believing in the philosophy that shelters should be a moment in someone's life journey and not a life sentence, all staff must be committed to the goal of assisting guests to exit well. Shelter staff direct guests to the support service staff who can begin the process of connecting guests to our Wellness Centre in downtown Calgary. There the magic happens.

When you step off one of our morning buses, you are dropped off next to our Wellness Centre. If we call the services at the shelter building "Essential Services," those at the Wellness Centre are "Care Services." The Centre has been open for almost two years, and its success has been staggering. We have gone from 700 interventions per month to almost 5,000. The Centre is in our twelve-storey residential building called the "1010 tower" — our largest housing project. It has 224 units, and almost everyone who is housed there was once homeless.

The Mustard Seed Wellness Centre helps clients prepare for life after homelessness.

Entering the Wellness Centre, you are greeted by a staff member, who is often assisted by a volunteer. The waiting area is clean and bright. A large television screen slowly scrolls through a menu detailing the Mustard Seed daily activities and services. An advocate calls your name and invites you to their office. There are four full-time advocates who assist with acquiring identification if yours is lost; filling out forms for Social Assistance; connecting you to a housing worker; making medical, dental, physical therapy, occupational therapy, chiropractic or massage appointments or introducing you to an addictions counselor, chaplain or any other service you may need. All of these services are housed in the Wellness Centre, but we also outsource.

While all services are free to Mustard Seed clients, the average cost of a service to our organization is just over $5 per visit, which is more than $120 less expensive than a traditional facility. This is possible for several reasons. Many professionals, like our chiropractors and massage therapists, volunteer their time. This is a huge gift, and we find many guests who have never experienced these services before. A local not-for-profit acts as a partner and shares one of its medical doctors, who has many years working with homeless and formerly homeless patients. Finally, our Clinical Director has made arrangements with several universities and colleges to use our centre for locums and practicum students. The Clinical Director, who is also a registered psychologist, gives careful oversight to this program; several students have graduated and returned to work with us full-time.

People who live in the 1010 tower or other Mustard Seed apartments, shelter users or those who are sleeping rough can access the Wellness Centre. The same building includes a full-service pharmacy. The pharmacist has worked with the homeless population for years and has spent time in our shelter. The level of care from him and his team is unsurpassed. He knows our guests by name. He carefully answers their questions. He works with our staff to ensure that they understand the purpose of a drug and its side effects.

We strongly believe that such an integrated service model is critical to support people to move from homeless to housed. We believe that people can be responsible for their own care plan and that we are partners with them on their journey. From our Exit Strategists in the shelter to Resident Engagement staff in our housing department, an integrated team approach keeps people supported and housed.

While we use a Permanent Supportive Housing (PSH) model, this does not mean that people will be with us forever. We keep track of both negative and positive move-outs. People die, go to jail, decide they are making enough money at their job to afford a bigger apartment or decide to move in with a friend; they may move on.

We have harm reduction, sober and dry buildings. This is important because not everyone is at the same place in their exit from homelessness. We also see eviction as a last resort. Everyone in our housing group is assigned to a Resident Engagement worker, and we have staff available 24/7. Rather than evicting, which absolves us of all future responsibility, we prefer to relocate. If our building is not right for someone, staff will work to find a more suitable accommodation. Sometimes people need more physical supports than we can provide. Sometimes a resident poses a threat to the rest of the building. We believe that evicting to homelessness is not an option.

Another very important component of our work is our Employment Team. There are many people who end up homeless who cannot work. I am always so grateful that we have social service programs available for them. In Alberta, one of our best programs is Assured Income for the Severely Handicapped (AISH), and it provides $1,588 per month. In our buildings, where rents range from $300 to $800 a month, AISH is enough for people to get by on. Coverage in Alberta may include financial and health benefits for dependents as well. Other available programs include Alberta Works. While these programs are extremely supportive, for most people, employment is the key to a successful future.

The Mustard Seed Employment Program has a staff of eight. They work exclusively with homeless and formerly homeless clients. It is astounding to think that in the first six months of 2018, their clients obtained over 200 jobs in Calgary. In addition to traditional counseling for clients, one of the program anchors is the Seed Academy. "Scholars" at the Academy come from shelter, the streets and our housing to spend a week in school. The school is held every other week and takes up to a dozen people. The instructor is very relational, and topics such as resume preparation, grooming and dealing with a criminal record are addressed. Experts are invited to spend time with the scholars, and employers often attend. This program is so successful that we plan to take it to other Mustard Seed city sites.

We also have employment counselors in off-site locations. We have a full-time and very busy counselor in one of our Community Hubs; another is situated at the Safe Communities Opportunity and Resource Centre (SORCe).[3] SORCe is a unique Calgary program with support staff from numerous community agencies, including Calgary Police Services, under one roof. To support our staff, the Employment Program has two new Mustard Seed–branded SUVs that staff use to transport clients to job interviews. Once a client obtains work, they do not graduate from the program until their employment is considered stable.

In his book *Early Intervention: How Canada's Social Programs Can Work Better, Save Lives, and Often Save Money*, James Hughes discusses the failures of the shelter system and the significant cost of keeping someone homeless.[4] Hughes helps us to see where we have gone wrong and how, through a Housing First supportive model, we can not only shelter people but move them to wellness. As I read this work, I felt it resonate with the model of care we've built at the Mustard Seed Wellness Centre. It is, in my humble view, the shelter's best future.

CHAPTER 10
Restoring Community
Karen Hoeft, Edmonton, AB

Introduction

My story begins in Regina, Saskatchewan, in 1961. I grew up in a large family with seven children. My parents, grandparents, siblings and I all lived together in Wartime Housing (Wartime Housing Corporation put up over 25,000 units across Canada between 1941 and 1944). In 1964, when we all moved to a 960-square foot bungalow, it seemed like a mansion to our family.

My parents attended church meetings at the Salvation Army, so many of my early memories are of open-air meetings downtown — singing and playing a brass instrument on "skid row." Our family often attended worship services at the Salvation Army's Men's Shelter. Even on Christmas Day, we would celebrate with the men who lived there. When some of these men came to church on Sundays, my parents invariably invited two or three of them home for dinner. One of these men would later become my father-in-law. So in many ways, homeless shelters have always been part of my life.

I was commissioned as a Salvation Army officer in 1987, and for twenty-one of the years since, I have been a shelter Director. I have served in High River, Alberta; Yellowknife, Northwest Territories; Winnipeg, Manitoba; Prince George, BC; Sudbury, Ontario; and now in Edmonton, Alberta. While my current Salvation Army posting is not in shelter management, I'm honoured to be sharing my vision for the future of sheltering based on my extensive cross-Canada experience in the field from my new Edmonton home base.

July, 2018: A barbeque where relocation and new building plans were announced to the residents of the Salvation Army's Addictions & Relocation Centre in Edmonton.

Community

Everyone begins life in a home. Our mother gives birth to us and — for the majority of us — we are raised in a family.

The home represents a place of safety, a place where an infant is cared for, loved and nurtured. The home is where we learn values and how to interact with others. It is multi-generational. It is a place where we belong.

A group of homes is called a community. Here we learn togetherness, understanding and a broader sense of belonging to the whole. In community, we find strength to face the world and all its challenges, to work together and thrive. In community, we see the gifts of individuals and families coming together to create something that will sustain life and build a solid foundation for future generations.

A homeless shelter is often required when the natural structures of community are changed, broken or destroyed. The shelter's goal is to work alongside the men and women who have no place else to turn and help them get back to community. I believe that the future of homeless sheltering is about reconnecting community to men and women who have become disconnected from it; in short, shelters should be focused on restoring community. This mission has two component parts. First, to provide people living in shelters the opportunity to rediscover themselves outside their identity as "homeless." Second, to help people with no home to find, settle into and retain their own housing in such a way that they never need to return to a shelter.

Beyond the label

I say that people live in homeless shelters, not that homeless people live in shelters. We need to intentionally see everyone who comes and stays in a shelter as a person first, and all too often, that's forgotten. This sounds basic, but it happens all the time — we refer to "the homeless." Community leaders and advocates come together to solve the problem of "the homeless" in their community. This label — "homeless" — comes with all kinds of baggage. People have a mental image of how a "homeless person" looks and acts. These are often negative stereotypes that represent only a small minority of the people who actually reside in emergency shelters in Canada.

So what could we call the people who stay in emergency shelters instead to reflect this lesson — clients, residents, patrons, guests? I propose that we call them *people*. We need to get to know their names. They are first and foremost human beings. They have personhood; they are individuals with thoughts, feelings, behaviours and history. They have a mother and a father (whether they know them or not), extended family — children, siblings, aunts, uncles, cousins, grandparents — and a family history. They have friends and neighbours, teachers and fellow students, former bosses and co-workers. They have a status in our country: citizen, landed immigrant, student, refugee, migrant and/or visitor. They love and are loved. They have values and characteristics that are deep and powerful.

I am always amazed when people are surprised if a person, who happens to be homeless, helps a stranger in distress. Such stories often make the headlines. Why are we surprised? Many people I have met on my journey in homeless shelters would give their life for mine if I were in danger.

They each have a name:

Brian, we cried together at the funeral of a common friend.

Christine, we talked about our clothes and how they reflect what we think about ourselves.

Joey, he taught me about pain and alcohol while we played cribbage.

Patricia, she always requested the same song and cried every time I sang it for her.

Ashley, who humbled me by his willingness to share his story so others could learn from it.

Edward, he could always get me to laugh.

Archie, who broke my heart when he passed away.

Doris, she reminded me that we were on the same journey as women, and

Bradley, he allowed me to speak on his behalf when he had no words left.

These people represent so many I have known. They were without homes, but they are so much more than "the homeless." Both inside and outside of homeless shelters we need to begin with language that acknowledges this, or we dehumanize and exclude the very people we are trying to include.

Let's start with the resolve that we will see each individual first as a person, who lives and breathes, feels happiness and sadness, acts out in caring ways and in frustrated ways, who get it right as well as makes mistakes. We need to do this for moral reasons but also for very practical ones. Shelters need to remind the people who flow through their facilities that they have abilities, skills and opinions and are able to contribute them to whatever community they eventually rejoin. Community expects members to give to it and not just take from it. Thus, job one at the shelter is to reconnect individuals to themselves in a way that empowers them to retake their full and legitimate place in community. When people who were once homeless are indeed able to take their place with the confidence they are the equal of those in the community, their risk of returning to the shelter is diminished dramatically.

Accordingly, every shelter needs to have the capacity to patiently listen to the stories of the people staying with them. Creating and maintaining a caring environment where the story can be told and helping the teller discover the beauty and potential it offers for a better life comprise professional competencies we need at shelters. I have come to recognize that story is the key. When we categorize or label people, we don't take time to hear their stories. Everyone has a story and they all are unique, but there are some common paths that can lead to being homeless and also to being housed. Sometimes in our haste to help people, we may assume we know their story. When we take the time to listen to another person's story, we validate their life experience and their journey. Their own story is the key that helps unlock the door to their future.

Understanding the journey into homelessness

Understanding the journey into the homeless shelter not only helps to re-empower people and prepare them for a future in community, it also can help the shelter team understand the best possible route out of homelessness and into homes. Each person's story is one-of-a-kind and worth hearing. Hearing people's stories over the years has made me rich beyond measure. In sharing their journeys with me, they have taught me the amazing resiliency of the human spirit.

The primary reason people present at a shelter is probably safety. They are not safe where they live, so they turn to an emergency shelter for protection — from other people, from the weather, from unsafe living conditions and many other circumstances.

Breakdowns in the family unit constitute another major reason people enter the shelter system. Young adults who, for various reasons, can't live with their parents any longer can find themselves needing an emergency shelter. They may have difficulty maintaining the cost of housing on low wages or have worn out their welcome at a friend's place.

When relationships break apart, people may end up in a shelter before they find another place to stay. Single parents often have limited resources when unforeseen events happen, which can put them at high risk for becoming homeless. Many people say they never thought they would need shelter services. People who become estranged from their families have no support when they fall on tough times and need help in a time of crisis, so they turn to an emergency shelter for their support network. People exiting the foster care system often end up in emergency shelters because they don't have any natural family support networks.

Emergency sheltering may be necessary because of a natural disaster, such as a fire or flood. Or it could be the result of longer-term trends, such as urbanization — as people move from rural farming or fishing communities to larger cities in search of job opportunities.

Intentional actions such as the *Indian Act*, creation of reserves, forced attendance at Indian Residential Schools and large-scale adoption out of Indigenous communities during the sixties "scoop" have destroyed communities, which has led to disproportionately high numbers of Indigenous people residing in shelters. When communities are splintered, the natural sense of belonging and support networks are lost. But they can be restored.

I met Isobel in downtown Winnipeg in 2008. Isobel was

over eighty, and she had spent the previous ten years living in an emergency shelter. Her old-age pension cheque was her only means of support, and she had no family to help her navigate the available housing options; she was stuck in the shelter system. In partnership with the Gerontology Department at Concordia Hospital, she and nine other people over seventy-five were assessed, and all were moved to long-term care facilities within a month. It was only because we knew Isobel's story and were able to share it with an institutional partner that we were successful in moving Isobel to safe, long-term housing.

A deep understanding of the difficult journey into homelessness can help staff to shape a housing option that addresses those causes. Listening and learning from a person's story can help staff identify the supports needed, how best to access them and the availability of appropriate housing with the necessary supports. Through the personal story, staff can recognize community gaps, bring awareness to the needs and advocate for appropriate bridges to help house people with multiple challenges in the right neighbourhood, with adequate support and with access to community-based connections.

The dangers of sheltering

There is great danger in not understanding the journey, not empowering people and not accompanying them as quickly as possible back to community — the natural cycle of human interaction can regress when one checks into — and stays too long in — the shelter system.

You can tell who has been in shelters too long. These are the people who expect meals to be served exactly on time. They line up for the meal; if the meal is late, they become impatient and may even leave in exasperation. They will complain to staff. I usually remind them that meals are not served on a precise schedule for most people in the world. In homes, meals are served when they are fully cooked and everyone has arrived. Frustration over late meals usually indicates that a person has become institutionalized.

In shelters, adults are too often asked to conform to more child-like behaviours of dependence and obedience. For example, there are usually specific wake-up times, meal times and lights out times. These are often governed by the need to clean rooms, serve meals and allow people to get a good night's sleep. Safety concerns and staffing ratios also play a role. However, most adults dislike being told they need to follow certain guidelines to stay in the shelter. These rules often feel restrictive to adults who have not had to answer for their behaviour in many years. They often feel like they are being treated like children. These feelings can lead to outbursts as they assert their independence. The longer people live in emergency shelters, the more likely they are to become institutionalized, and the harder it is for them to move back into community and interdependent living.

When a person first checks into a shelter, they are often thankful to have a place to stay. The longer they remain, however, the more likely they are to become frustrated with the guidelines. The natural response when an adult is asked to regress to child-like guidelines is to fight for independence. This can manifest in behaviours that lead shelters to restrict people from staying there, because violence cannot be tolerated. Organizations that run emergency shelters, like all organizations and enterprises, are obligated by law to protect workers from violence. They also need to provide a safe place for all the other people living in the shelter. When people live in shelters for a long period of time, they become institutionalized and cannot cope without specific wake-up calls, rigid meal times and other structures in place — the same phenomenon seen in prisons and long-term residential care. This is why we must ensure that people stay in shelters as short a time as possible.

Many shelters do impose time limits on stays because of the volume of people they serve, requirements set by contracts or funders or because they have limited resources and are trying to help as many people as possible. Length of stay can also be mandated by provincial or territorial law.

A long shelter stay is never a good thing. We do not want emergency shelters to become places where people are institutionalized; rather, we want to help them reach the stage of interdependence by supporting them on their journey to being housed. Ultimately, we hope to use emergency shelters only for emergencies.

The journey out of homelessness

As people present at shelters and we start to learn their story, we are able to support them in their journey to being housed. This should be the second main mandate of the shelter.

From a housing perspective, the emergency shelter is analogous to an emergency department in a hospital. A person presents at an emergency department because he or she is in a medical crisis that requires immediate attention. Their information is taken and they are seen by a health practitioner, who then takes a fuller history and assesses the situation. There are many potential outcomes. They could have a series of tests to help discover what is wrong. They could have surgery, be given a prescription and sent home or they could stay in the emergency department until a bed opens up in a ward. They will often have follow-up appointments with their family physician after returning home from the hospital. The emergency department is where people are identified, triaged and then sent to another location: a ward, operating room, another facility or home. The triage procedure identifies the next steps that need to be taken in each case.

In an emergency shelter setting, a person needs immediate protection from the outside elements. They present at a shelter, and as discussed above, their story is heard (similar to giving a history to the medical professional in the hospital analogy). We then begin the process of supporting them as they find their way back to being housed. If a person presents with limited capacity to make decisions, then there may be a need to find supports fairly quickly, or it may be determined that they cannot be supported in a shelter setting. For example, if they are in a medical crisis, they would need to be sent to a hospital; if they are at risk of harming themselves (suicidal) or others (violence), they are often required to have those issues dealt with by a mental health specialist or some other appropriate manner.

The emergency shelter's goals involve: 1) identifying someone's housing needs, and 2) providing temporary shelter until they are adequately housed. The emergency shelter is not the solution for housing in the long term, just as the emergency department is not the solution for ongoing health care needs.

We look at housing along a continuum; this includes market home ownership, market rental housing, subsidized housing, supportive housing and finally transitional housing. Many variations exist on the spectrum, but this list captures the broad picture. Our job involves working with housing experts along the full continuum to ascertain the best housing option possible based on the best interest of the person in question. We can only achieve this goal by knowing both the person and the housing setting that will best represent community for that person. This, of course, is far easier said than done. Acting as a bridge between the individuals and their future communities is hard work — largely because of the short supply of appropriate, accessible and affordable housing in welcoming communities in Canada.

Bottlenecks

People leaving emergency shelters have very limited options for permanent housing. I saw this early in life with my Uncle Hughie. Hughie lived in an old shack in rural Saskatchewan, near my grandparents' homestead. I can remember going out to his small farm to pick the vegetable harvest that he would share with us. Eventually, he could no longer cut enough wood to last the winter season, and he moved into Regina during the winters. He lodged at an old hotel on Rose Street where I had played with the Salvation Army bands in my youth (we now call such establishments Single Resident Occupancy Hotels or SROs). In the summers he moved back to the farm and planted his garden. One year he wasn't able to get back out to the farm. We received a call informing us that Uncle Hughie was in hospital because there had been a fire at the SRO where he was staying. He had lost everything — even his false teeth! This fiercely independent Scotsman was now homeless.

While my uncle's story is deeply personal, I have seen commonalities in many other people's stories. In the Canadian North I met many people who, like my Uncle Hughie, had lived "on the land." Many had lived a subsistence lifestyle, which included hunting, fishing and trapping; they had amazing stories of survival in the bush. Yet as they grew older and could no longer sustain that lifestyle, they came into town and often lived in an SRO. Yellowknife had the Gold Range; Winnipeg, the McLaren Hotel and the Manwin; Sudbury, the Frood Hotel. As I write this, the Balmoral Hotel is being closed down in Vancouver's Downtown Eastside, displacing 142 people. When these hotels are finally declared "unsafe for human habitation," burn down or get sold and torn down, they displace many people, who then often find themselves at emergency shelters. The people who live in these SROs across our country each have a story. Many of them, like my Uncle Hughie, had lived independently, and if we had more adequate and affordable housing available, they would not need to go to emergency shelters.

Everyone knows that the cost of housing has increased in our country, however, we often don't connect the housing market with emergency shelters. We need to talk about how to build enough homes for all the people who live in Canada. As SROs close down, they are not being replaced with the same amount of affordable housing, so availability becomes a major issue. We simply do not have enough subsidized housing units for people to move into, and their present income sources often keep them out of market rental units.

SROs usually occupy high density buildings, meaning one building houses a lot of people. Today's zoning laws usually limit the number of units that can be constructed in a set space, so most new housing builds are lower density and therefore often carry higher costs. The cost of building structures that meet all the health and safety requirements is significant, and without government subsidies, tax incentives or a charitable organization fundraising to support a building, low income people — including people who have needed the services of a homeless shelter — will continue to face serious difficulties accessing housing.

Affordability raises another huge issue. Housing should not cost more than 30 per cent of before-tax household income.

This guideline is intended to leave people with enough income to use for food, transportation, taxes, clothes and other necessities. For a person working full-time (thirty-five hours per week) at minimum wage ($10.45 per hour average in Canada), "affordable" according to this standard would mean a rent of approximately $475 per month. Not many rental units exist at this rate unless they need major repairs.

In 2017, the federal government concluded a discussion called "Let's Talk Housing" that involved engaging Canadians to help shape Canada's National Housing Strategy. We need to be involved in the discussion, not just for ourselves and what kind of housing we need, but also for all people in our country. It may be your uncle or aunt, your niece or nephew who ends up needing a shelter bed because we haven't looked after the housing needs of all Canadians.

Conclusion

Sometimes the way out has already been found; we do not always have to find new ways — we can learn from our past. General William Booth, co-founder of the Salvation Army, wrote these words back in 1890, and they still resonate today:

> *As I have repeatedly stated already, but will state once more, for it is important enough to bear endless repetition, one of the first steps which must inevitably be taken in the reformation of this class, is to make for them decent, healthy, pleasant homes, or help them to make them for themselves, which, if possible, is far better. I do not regard the institution of any first, second, or third-class lodging-houses as affording anything but palliatives of the existing distress. To substitute*

life in a boarding-house for life in the streets is, no doubt, an immense advance, but it is by no means the ultimatum. Life in a boarding-house is better than the worst, but it is far from being the best form of human existence. Hence, the object I constantly keep in view is how to pilot those persons who have been set on their feet again by means of the Food and Shelter Depots, and who have obtained employment in the city, into the possession of homes of their own. (William Booth, In Darkest England and the Way Out, *1890, p. 210)*

We need to come together as a community and as a country to work on real solutions to house Canadians. During World War II we found a creative solution to a housing shortage in Canada with Wartime Housing. This will not be the solution for today, but it gives us hope that what we have done before, we can do again. When we, the voting citizens of our country, decide that this is truly a priority for our country, as big if not bigger than our health care issues, we will see change. We will see neighbourhoods redeveloped to include all income levels, zoning bylaws changed to include smaller-footprint homes and enough homes for all who live in our great country, including those who find themselves homeless.

In the last fifteen years we have had more conversation and many conferences about the role of shelters in community. We have questioned whether we really need them, or whether we might eliminate them entirely. I believe that the role shelters play has become more significant than ever.

As in the example of a hospital emergency department, it is critical to understand the person's full story. This will take training so that front-line staff (usually some of the lowest paid positions in the whole social service field) will know how to take time to hear the story, understand it, and make informed decisions based on it. This is often called a "trauma-informed approach." It means that we will need highly skilled teams, like trauma teams in hospitals, to respond quickly so that the impact of being homeless is contained and, if possible, quickly reversed. This will need to be done in a myriad of ways because remote, rural and urban communities have different capacities and different challenges; however, it will need to be a multi-disciplined, cross-sector approach. A "trauma-like" team will need to respond to whoever walks in the door, because no two people are exactly the same.

Although "homeless shelters" may be required when the natural structures of community are changed, broken or destroyed, there is a way forward. As citizens and as a nation we can listen to and learn from the people who have had to take refuge in a shelter and also from people who have operated or worked in those shelters. Together we can forge a path that will benefit not only those individuals who may face the challenge of homelessness, but also build stronger, more resilient communities for future generations.

Future homeless shelters will help the people who dwell there rebuild both their sense of community and their ability to function within one. I suggest they will succeed in fulfilling this mission if they value individuals, listen to their stories, identify their individual needs and work to avoid institutionalization. Homeless shelters must be a stepping stone to a place the people they serve can really call "home" and avoid at all costs seeing themselves as the solution. Then and only then will they fulfill their role as a place where people are restored to their rightful place in community.

CHAPTER 11
Decolonizing the North
Arlene Haché, Yellowknife, NT

This chapter explores the provision of sheltering services in the Canadian North from my perspective as a person who was homeless and lived in an emergency shelter. It also references my experience as a founder and operator of a Yellowknife-based emergency shelter for women who were homeless, the majority of whom were First Nations, Inuit and Métis. Finally, it presents findings and recommendations of a 2015 study I initiated in which women with lived experience of homelessness were asked to discuss how services could more effectively support them in moving from the emergency shelter and transitional housing to the community.

Living homeless
I hitchhiked from a small farming community in southern Ontario to the Northwest Territories when I was nineteen

years old. I had dropped out of college and therefore was no longer allowed to stay in the student residence. Life at home had been vicious from childhood, so going home was out of the question. I couldn't imagine the outcome if I went home and told my parents that I had dropped out. Instead, I spent some time in the city park tucked under the bushes to sleep before I decided to head west on Highway 401. I hung out at the local hotels, slipping into big conferences and gatherings to sneak food and on Sundays hoped to get an invitation to lunch after church. I lived in self-imposed isolation, too afraid and ashamed to tell anyone what was going on.

The week-long journey to Yellowknife was uneventful, and the people who gave me rides were generous in making sure I had food to eat. When I reached Edmonton, I checked in with the Salvation Army where the staff bought me a bus ticket to go the rest of the way because they were concerned for my safety. In Yellowknife, I stayed at the emergency shelter for women operated by the YWCA until I met a family at church that took me into their home. The family was incredibly kind and supportive, but I eventually wore out my welcome. I returned to the shelter often, paying a small nightly fee to access the service. We were able to eat meals, and the staff didn't get into my business, which I appreciated because it made me feel safe.

I flitted from job to job in Yellowknife, never keeping one for more than three months at a time because of my own insecurities and lack of self-confidence. At one point, I had held and walked out on so many jobs, I ducked in and out of stores and buildings to hide from former employers — I didn't want to run into them and have to explain why I had disappeared. One employer reported me as a missing person to the RCMP when I didn't show up to work for a couple of days. The RCMP cornered me in an elevator to ask my name and then proceeded to tell me my boss was worried about me. I was embarrassed and reacted by yelling at them to tell my boss to mind his own business, but underneath it all I was surprised and mystified that anyone would bother to look for me. As far as I knew, my family hadn't bothered to search for me, and I hadn't spoken to them in years.

Even though I was excruciatingly shy and insecure, I made a lot of friends as I flip-flopped between bars, church groups and support groups trying to find some sign I was of value to somebody. Loneliness, desperation and an insatiable need for love translated into many one-night stands. With some men who were simply trying to be nice to me, I responded in a sexualized way that targeted them. In my single-minded drive to please people and get their approval, I hid who I was behind lies and deception, big and small, and with every angry reaction and confrontation, inevitably my deceptive and harmful behaviour deepened. I lived my life out as a victim ruled by a sense of powerlessness and hopelessness grasping to fulfill needs that could never be met because they relied on outside relief from other people. Even though people who were trying to help me talked about the importance of personal responsibility, I did not internalize the connection between decisions I was making and outcomes I was experiencing. Suicide was on my mind almost constantly, and I thought I was simply a crazy person who wasn't meant to make it. I learned later that I was suffering from severe clinical depression and post-traumatic stress disorder because of the psychological, physical and sexual abuse I had experienced as a child and teen.

The greatest comfort came from conversations with people who shared similar experiences — we propped each other up with affirmations of value we couldn't grant ourselves. Church friends tended to be more judgmental in their support, offering hope but also criticism, offering prayer as the sole change agent.

In comparison, non-faith support groups offered helpful information and skill-building options (though they rarely panned out in terms of real and tangible opportunities). The most effective recovery model from my experience came in a therapeutically based Life Skills program developed in the 1980s. The Life Skills program acknowledged victimization and impacts of trauma but asked participants to try to set the past aside in order to focus on developing functional abilities, personal responsibility, clear communication skills and decision-making capacity. It was empowering to discover that life doesn't just happen but that I have a right and a responsibility to make my own decisions.

Colonial constructs of homelessness

Ultimately, marriage and the stability of my husband got me off the street and into a permanent home. My confidence and capacity to contribute to the community increased as I became more self-reflective and knowledgeable — and as I gained a broader set of personal and professional skills. By 1990, sixteen years after I had arrived in the Northwest Territories, I, along with several other women, founded a new equity-seeking women's group to address a perception held by many that the existing local women's organizations were marginalizing and not representative of their experiences or interests. Members tasked the newly formed Yellowknife Women's Society with supporting local women and helping them empower themselves so they could develop their own goals, achieve wellness, enjoy equality and gain recognition for their contributions to the community. They chose a unique, consensus-style governance model that envisioned a North where women's voices are unfettered;

cultural diversity is nurtured and celebrated; and women live healthy, empowered lives that are enriching to their families and communities.

Shortly thereafter, the Society established the Yellowknife Women's Centre, situated in a small rented house. I worked at the Centre in a full-time, volunteer capacity for four years and became its first Executive Director in 1995, when we secured short-term project funding to deliver a pre-natal nutrition program and a training and employment program for women.

Almost all the participants were First Nations, Inuit and Métis, so by default the organization fell into an advocacy role — working to combat a dehumanizing colonial ideology that served to destroy every aspect of the lives of these women and their families. The Society became a steadfast and long-standing member of several coalitions and partnerships, including the Yellowknife Homelessness Coalition and the Northwest Territories Coalition Against Family Violence. While collaborative efforts resulted in some excellent outcomes, our ally relationships with both coalitions as well as funder and political entities were often strained by the Centre's advocacy positions because these positions called their policies and practices into question.

Contemporary social services delivery models established to support First Nations, Inuit and Métis women are inexorably linked to a worldview that refuses to separate patriarchy and gender violence from colonialism and racism (Smith & Ross, 2004). Women are forced from their homes and communities into the city and regional centres by poverty, lack of access to services, overcrowded housing and epidemic rates of violence, both internal and external to the Indigenous community. Isolated from the support of friends and families, women face daily experiences of systemic racism and institutional betrayal that cost them dearly in terms of their own well-being and that of their children. Christensen (2012) and Neal (2004) concluded that shelter environments inherently generate dependency and result in institutionalization. Neal (2004) concluded that women are reduced "to a marginal place where they learn to work their way through the shelter system by using these services with deference and gratitude" (p. 28).

That is not to say shelters are not viewed as critical nor valued by the women. Neal determined that the shelter offered the safest environment some of the women had found. Four Worlds Centre for Development (2007) concurred, saying an adequate support system made the difference for Northern women at risk of becoming homeless. Four Worlds found that informal support systems often failed because women were forced to leave their communities for safety reasons or to access services, or situations were too stressful for families and friends already under a strain from the impacts of intergenerational trauma. Neal stated that the women viewed shelters as places of assistance and developed positive relationships with the staff, some of them becoming friends. On the other hand, relationships could be strained due to lack of adequate funding, overworked and overzealous workers and volunteers and cultural misunderstandings.

Despite the service's value, women felt they paid a price when forced to comply with restrictive rules and regulations, even if for their own safety (Neal, 2004). Neal found that the regimented atmosphere of a shelter replicated environments the women had fled. The Four Worlds study demonstrated that many service providers operated from a dogmatic position of punishment, exclusion, inflexibility and societal indifference toward homeless people. For example, Neal gave the example of women being excluded from family violence shelters because of alcohol on their breath. "In general, the respondents do not perceive that these agencies, and their employees, are interested in helping them or will do anything other than make their already difficult lives more unbearable" (Four Worlds Centre for Development, p. xix). Webster (2006) supported those findings, stating that "strong systemic pressures and prejudices" (p. 24) existed among community members and service providers in the North. Webster stated, "Blaming and shunning victims — including homeless people — and denying services were cited as significant obstacles" (p. 24).

In Canada, two primary housing options are being considered by stakeholders as most effective in meeting the needs of people who are experiencing homelessness: the Continuum of Care model and the Housing First Model (Falvo, 2008; Klodawsky, 2009). Both Falvo and Klodawsky credited the generation of Housing First to the failures of the Continuum of Care model. The Continuum of Care model assumes individuals who are homeless, especially those with severe mental health and addiction issues, are incapable of living in regular housing without onsite support (Falvo, 2008; Klodawsky, 2009). Falvo described the model as a "lengthy and arduous audition" (p. 32) that holds people who are homeless to a standard of behaviour judged by service providers as either ready to transition into a housing alternative or not. Depending on readiness, homeless individuals move from the shelter to transitional housing to semi-permanent or permanent housing. Some housing providers demand alcohol abstention as part of that package and either reward compliance or punish non-compliance of any condition with delayed housing or eviction. As reflected in the comments above, homeless individuals found the conditions "onerous and unrealistic" (Falvo, 2008, p. 32), and there was some question about the efficacy of using those criteria to assess housing readiness.

In my advocacy role, I witnessed workers punishing residents for attitudes and behaviours that were in keeping with their worldview and experiences but were deemed problematic by the institution. It was especially difficult for Indigenous women who struggled to understand and comply with rules and expectations that were counterintuitive to their ways of knowing and being in community. Some women tried to fight back but inevitably ran up against rigid and coercive administrative and legal systems. Others responded with feelings of powerlessness and gratitude for being allowed to survive. In this context, two brave women come to mind (whose names I will not disclose to protect them from unwanted attention).

Advocacy by shelter activists for better services and more safety for women in Yellowknife.

The first is a Tłįchǫ woman from the Northwest Territories who won the first United Nations judgment against Canada under the Convention on the Elimination of All Forms of Discrimination against Women (CEDAW) for racism and discrimination. In that instance, the tribunal found that the Government of the Northwest Territories (GNWT) had illegally removed her name from home ownership papers at the request of her ex-partner, which resulted in her becoming homeless. Seven lawyers and fifteen years later, the case was lost in the Canadian civil courts because her lawyers had failed to move the matter forward in a timely manner. She eventually found justice outside the country in an international forum, but the Government of Canada refuses to comply with the recommendations.

The second is an Inuk woman who lost her job at a family violence shelter when she was hospitalized after a vicious attack by her partner. The woman was thankful her employer had written a letter explaining the situation to Employment Insurance, not realizing they had actually terminated her from a position she had held for five years. No one from the shelter or her colleagues contacted her to find out if she was okay or how she was doing, and she never returned to work at that organization.

Smith and Ross (2004) suggested that a reliance on government funding constituted a persuasive factor in civil society relationships where agencies worked with government to implement colonial policies and practices rather than making it accountable. Christensen (2012) concurred, asserting shelter and transitional housing service providers operated from a colonial construct because funding parameters instituted by the Government of the Northwest Territories required it. I have a slightly different take. In my view, service providers in the North actively lobby decision-makers to maintain the *status quo* regardless of the harm it causes Indigenous Peoples because an anti-rights approach to housing and homelessness solidifies their power and supports a corporate, empire-building agenda. Survival as an organization takes prominence over the survival of women they claim to serve, and gaslighting tactics are used to make women question their reality and their value.

Sheltering in the North

Shortly after the Yellowknife Women's Centre opened, a disabled woman was kicked out of her housing unit by the YWCA because she smoked and experienced blackouts from epileptic episodes. They said the eviction was initiated because the woman posed a risk to herself and others. I couldn't imagine a greater risk to her than blacking out on a street in the dead of winter, so we agreed to let her sleep on the couch in our office until we could find a more permanent solution. Over the subsequent fifteen years, other First Nations, Inuit and Métis women came to sleep on our office floors and couches, either because they couldn't or wouldn't access the emergency shelter or transition housing services operated by the YWCA. In 2005, the GNWT responded to the inhumane living conditions of the women living in the basement of the Centre by granting our organization access to a large, empty building that had been previously used as a detox centre.

The move into the new building and formalization of emergency shelter services offered by the Centre shifted the funding source from allocations under the GNWT Health and Social Services Family Violence budget to the GNWT Education, Cultural and Employment Income Support budget. The emergency shelter could accommodate up to nine women but was funded for sixteen beds. On average, twenty-five to thirty women accessed sheltering services every night, the majority of them sleeping on three-inch mats on the floor. The Centre, like other emergency shelters, was funded at a rate of $42 per bed night; we received $272,000 in annual funding. By contrast, the YWCA operated a twelve-bed family violence shelter funded at a rate of $173 per bed night, receiving roughly $700,000 in annual funding. Women in the family violence shelter received a monthly comfort allowance to cover basic needs, but women who were homeless did not. And although both shelters were located in buildings owned by the GNWT, the Centre was required to pay $3,200 a month in rent while the YWCA paid no rent. When the time came to build a new transition house specifically for women living in the emergency shelter, decades of underfunding and debt prohibited the Centre from taking on the project. The YWCA, positioned as the more stable and capable organization, stepped up and then promptly asserted a family violence housing mandate that excluded women staying in the homeless shelter from accessing the new transition house.

Neal (2004) asserted that homelessness defined and marginalized women more than any other descriptor, including poor mental health, addictions or disabilities. The arbitrary delineation between women experiencing violence and women experiencing homelessness embraced by decision-makers and the disparity in the allocation of resources led to a stigmatizing narrative that they were different; actually, depending on the moment and the day, these were the very same women.

Christensen (2012) found that both housing and employment policies and practices in the North relied on the concepts of "deserving" and "undeserving" at their core, thus marginalizing the homeless as deviant. That marginalization was reinforced by the family violence shelter movement, which refused to provide services to women who smelled of alcohol, who exhibited certain forms of mental illness or who failed to comply with multitudes of rules that were often in direct opposition to how women living in community experienced life. One First Nations woman said she should have stayed with her ex-partner instead of going to the family violence shelter because he didn't harass her as much as the workers. Several Indigenous women refused to go to the shelter because they were afraid the workers would call child welfare on them. One Inuk woman who moved into public housing after having lived in transitional housing for several years said it felt like she had just been released from a very long jail sentence.

This two-tiered system was further entrenched by punishing reactions from decision-makers and "allies" who viewed the advocacy efforts of the Yellowknife Women's Society to address social justice issues as divisive and combative. They appeared ignorant of the herculean effort it took to maintain collaborative relationships in the face of rampant racism, sexism and classism — served on a platter of white privilege and wrapped in a froth of white fragility. As well, the peer-led nature of the Centre was mischaracterized by decision-makers and allies, who portrayed it as an agency that was less knowledgeable and less capable of meeting the needs of women and their families — even though it applied an evidence-based family support model in its service delivery. The Centre found this assertion ironic given that we housed and supported women that the family violence shelter, the hospital and correctional services refused to accommodate because they lacked the expertise and capacity. A First Nation woman consistently gaslighted by allies once said, "I can go with the flow most of the time, but when they want me to question my own intelligence I have to call it a day on the relationship."

This overlay is important in understanding the calculated nature of more recent lobbying efforts made by Women's Shelter Canada, a national association that claims to represent a "unified voice for women's shelters and transition houses in Canada." When it formed, Women's Shelter Canada made the deliberate decision to exclude women's shelters that supported homeless women. At the time they declared their clientele involved women fleeing violence, not women who were homeless. However, with the increased commitment of federal and provincial/territorial resources toward addressing homelessness, Women's Shelter Canada decided to flip its position. Now it proclaims that women fleeing violence are homeless by default and so they should be able access homelessness funding in addition to the funding they receive from the health portfolios.

Homelands without shelter

The Government of Canada and its colonial agents, including mainstream civil society and charitable organizations, have served to dispossess Indigenous Peoples of their lands, homes, language, culture, customs, wealth and governance systems. The outcome of that genocide revealed in devastating social impacts for Indigenous Peoples has until recently been cast by those colonial bodies as a nothing more than populations of flawed individuals lacking the capacity to live independently without their assistance. Decision-makers saw people who needed services as deviants who were unwilling or unable to help themselves rather than who they actually were, namely people forced by racist, sexist and classist systems into structured poverty, homelessness and violence. This persistent misrepresentation can only be corrected through the application of a human rights framework.

Christensen (2012) credited historic colonial systems playing out in contemporary power structures, including the sheltering system, for perpetuating the institutionalization of First Nations, Inuit and Métis Peoples experiencing homelessness. Métis scholar Jesse Thistle (2017), who himself rose like a phoenix from the ashes of homelessness, defined Indigenous homelessness as

> *a human condition that describes First Nations, Métis and Inuit individuals, families or communities lacking stable, permanent, appropriate housing, or the immediate prospect, means or ability to acquire such housing.*

First Nations, Inuit and Métis women living in the emergency shelter presented a collage of personalities that revealed strength, courage, compassion and humour. They were very committed to their families and maintained a keen sense of community within their own cultural contexts, which varied for every nation and community within the nations. The women had a strong spiritual base. As a woman struggling myself with the disabling impacts of trauma related to violence and homelessness, I found a family and home. It wasn't until I witnessed testimonies at the Truth and Reconciliation Commission (TRC) hearings that I more fully understood the genocide that had occurred and how I was positioned in that reality as a non-Indigenous woman working in Indigenous communities. Churchill (2002), Fasta and Collin-Vézina (2010) and Stannard (1992) compared the experience and survivor impacts of Indigenous Peoples in Canada to the holocaust perpetrated against the Jewish people. In light of the TRC Calls to Action, leaders — especially non-Indigenous leaders — need to examine the efficacy of their services in meeting the needs of Indigenous communities.

Decolonizing

In 2015, the Yellowknife Women's Centre supported my request to organize facilitated learning circles to find out how women living in the emergency shelter could be better supported in transitioning to the community. The year before, three women had transitioned from the emergency shelter to the community, with one of them moving into an apartment with her partner and two of them moving into the Salvation Army supported-living program for individuals experiencing mental illness. Three other women secured housing in the private market on their own. Within months, both women at the Salvation Army were evicted from the program and returned to the emergency shelter without notice and without a support plan in place.

Eleven women participated in the discussions, with one person identifying herself as Métis, four identifying as First Nations and six as Inuit. I grouped the results under four topics, namely "Culture, strength and resilience;" "Reflection, reclamation, and transformation;" "Advocacy, shared experience and emotional maturity" and "Homelessness to Home." Space prevents me from speaking to all of these areas so I'll limit myself to the fourth.

After experiencing homelessness, women who were housed found their sense of safety and well-being increased substantially, as did their level of independence. One woman said, "You have your own bed to rest in, and you don't need to go to someone else's bed." Still homelessness had resulted in traumatizing effects that were palpable and long lasting.

One woman said that in spite of being housed for sixteen years, she remains on high alert in case she is threatened with being tossed out. She said, "I look at myself and think I'm one of the lucky ones that got out of there." All of the women desperately wanted to dissuade others, especially young people, from following in their footsteps.

The high cost of living, especially housing, juxtaposed against the lack of job opportunities in small communities, combined with family breakdown, poverty and migration into the city contributed to homelessness. Although some of the women were on permanent disability as a result of chronic addictions, they all considered education, training and employment as essential aspects of being independent. Participants had worked hard from the time they were children, on the land and in residential school. Some had supported themselves from the time they were teenagers, paying their own rent and food. One woman said, "I got really tired of being woken up to go to school when I've been scrubbing diapers until five or six o'clock in the morning."

The work ethic they learned as children and youth carried over into their work situations and voluntary efforts at the shelter and other non-profits, but addictions and traumatic responses to stress reduced their ability to be present and consistent. Some women went to adult upgrading and took part in training programs they found life changing but did not get jobs at the end. Some women at the shelter sold crafts, while others had casual jobs at just above minimum wage. The women concluded that the Centre should offer a structured on-the-job training program with paid positions in the agency so residents could parlay those skills, talents and experiences into employment and careers in the community. A woman stated, "You get proud of what you've got and what you're made of when you have a job."

The emergency shelter was bottlenecked by a lack of housing and therefore functioned as permanent housing. Very few affordable housing options were available to the women, with one participant saying it took her five years to access subsidized housing. Debt, especially money owed to housing, was a universal challenge faced by the participants, and while government financial assistance programs were in place, the eligibility criteria and intake processes were complex and restrictive. The private market landlord, operating as a monopoly in the North, also refused to rent to anyone on financial assistance or on disability. Financial assistance did not extend to women who were couch surfing, as they did not have a permanent address, nor did it apply to shelter residents because funding to the agency was considered by the government to be the substitute for individualized support.

The Yellowknife Women's Centre's harm-reduction approach to sheltering was seen as enabling by some people, while the more regimented approach taken by the YWCA transition house was seen as punitive. The difference in philosophy and service modality frustrated relationships and inhibited collaborative approaches to transition planning. As a result, evictions from the transition house had women cycling back through the shelter without a referral or follow-up plan in place. One woman compared her move from the shelter to the transition house as that of going from a prison to a halfway house. The woman was hospitalized during the timespan she was at both facilities and credited those living conditions with being the cause for her nervous breakdown. She said, "It's like I said to myself, I am going to fail." The women recommended the City of Yellowknife and the Centre work with them to establish transition or co-op housing and suggested looking at an empty treatment facility outside of the city to lessen the distractions. One woman said, "When there is a bar just a couple of blocks away, I don't think there is anything that can help."

The primary success factors of women who had moved from the shelter to the community can be summarized as follows:

- While First Nations, Inuit and Métis women are distinct in their identities, as a collective, they draw upon a connection to the land, Indigenous culture and shared survivor experience to transition from the shelter.
- Women who transitioned from the shelter engaged in a personal journey of self-discovery to recover from post-traumatic stress responses related to colonization, systemic and internalized racism and sexualized gender violence.
- An advocate provided a key resource for women transitioning from the shelter to the community, as did the support of positive and trusted family members, friends and service providers.
- Transitioning from the shelter is only possible with alternative housing options and financial resources to cover monthly housing costs and other basic living needs.

These four success factors led me to propose four recommendations to inform the shelter's focus:

- Engage and mentor women representing the diversity of the homeless population in leadership opportunities, offering them multiple avenues for input into the shelter's operation.

- Develop and implement a culturally sound, competency-based staff training curriculum specific to the needs of the agency, and recruit First Nations, Inuit and Métis with lived experience of homelessness for those positions.
- Apply the post-traumatic stress response model developed by Mitchell and Maracle (2005) to design and deliver a culturally competent peer support and living skills program with an on-the-land component led by Elders.
- Separate intoxicated women from those who are sober and explore potential off-site transition and permanent housing options for the women.

Conclusion

I acknowledge the fact that other people will have a different perspective than the one I present in this chapter. I held the executive director position for the Yellowknife Women's Society for two decades. A 2011 stakeholder survey found that the Yellowknife Women's Centre was valued as a critical community service with the "unique capability to reach out to and support a group of people that rarely access other services." At the same time, it revealed a demand for a change in leadership at the Executive Director level, both to rejuvenate the organization, giving it a "fresh start," and to free it from a long history of controversy rooted in advocacy positions taken by the Centre decision-makers and allies that were considered adversarial. One survey participant stated that advocacy "gets the Centre in trouble sometimes" (p. 12) and another concluded that structural advocacy was not a good mix with program delivery. I take the position that it is unethical to ride the gravy train of the industry generated by poverty, homelessness and violence if you aren't prepared to put your neck on the line.

In 2009, I received the Order of Canada for my work to address social justice issues in the North, across Canada and globally. In 2012, the year I retired, I received the Queen Elizabeth II Diamond Jubilee Medal. I note these acknowledgments because although receiving them was a disjointed, surreal experience, I want to encourage other street and community leaders not to buy into the false myth that they are valueless.

Advocates and activists must stay alert to the gaslighting and co-opting efforts of those invested in maintaining the *status quo*. I currently serve under the guidance of an Elders Council and remain committed to the self-determination efforts of First Nations, Inuit and Métis. I have lobbied decision-makers to link funding to service providers that give voice and decision-making power to people with lived experience because they have an inside track on concrete and sustainable solutions to homelessness.

CHAPTER 12

Addressing Crisis

Trudi Shymka, Vancouver, BC

With so much happening to address homelessness through housing programs and support strategies, the question of what the future holds for shelters is timely.

Shelters do so much more than just respond to homelessness; they respond to crisis, and unfortunately crisis is part of the human condition. Twenty-five years ago, I came to the Downtown Eastside as a child and youth worker at a women's shelter. I wanted to work with children who were experiencing the crisis of homelessness and help them to cope and move through that challenging time.

I felt at the time that easing their passage through crisis could make a real difference in diminishing their suffering and helping them to thrive once they moved out. What I learned was that homelessness was only a small part of the challenges they were facing. Their shelter stay was only a

brief period of time in lives that had already been challenging before they came and continued to be once they
left. As I worked to understand the complexities and challenges women and their children faced, I hoped to make a
difference in their lives. Currently, I work as the Associate
Executive Director of The Bloom Group. I continue to learn
more every day about the violations — physical, economic
and emotional — that women have faced historically and
continue to face today.

Women in crisis

While homelessness constitutes a serious crisis for individuals faced with no place to live, housing does not address the
whole issue. Homelessness is often only part of a person's
story, only a symptom of complex challenges and circumstances that have produced a crisis. Crises can arise from
negative personal experiences, limited opportunities, health
challenges and often some form of discrimination. Shelters
are an important and beneficial part of responding to individuals in crisis, limiting negative impacts through accessible
and effective measures. Shelters have been, and will continue
to be, an integral part of the response to crisis and an effective way for society to embrace its responsibility to care for
those who are most vulnerable.

Gender inequality is omnipresent in our society: in poli-
tics, economics, religion, media, cultural norms and the
workplace, giving men more social power than women in
every sphere. This leads to greater vulnerability for women
and women with children, which is then exacerbated in times
of crisis. To best address social equality and safety needs in
light of this reality, women-only shelters are required.

Anne arrived at the shelter escorted by police, having been
assaulted by her boyfriend. This was not the first time this had

happened and was not her first experience staying in our shelter. Anne arrived as a mother of three children, all of whom had been placed in care. They shared an apartment with her boyfriend who was the father of the children. The boyfriend was sometimes violent, and when Anne had finally called the police to report his violence toward her, she and her children were removed from the home — not the boyfriend — for their own safety. Once in the shelter, Anne found herself without an income, three young children to care for and unable to find a home she could afford once she secured income assistance. Having run out of time at the shelter and on her boyfriend's promise of a better relationship, Anne decided to reunite the family and hope that things would go better. This cycle repeated many times until the authorities determined that the children were in danger of harm from Anne's boyfriend and were removed from her care. In effect, the government had accused Anne of not protecting her children from harm. Each time Anne returned to the shelter, she was more traumatized. The impact of this cycle of hopelessness multiplied both for her and her children.

While women are underrepresented in homeless counts, we know that women and children are particularly vulnerable to the kind of crisis that can lead to homelessness. They generally have fewer assets and are more likely to have jobs with limited, if any, employment security. In a crisis, they may be highly vulnerable to violence and exploitation.

We also know that many women and women with children will avoid shelters. This may stem from fear of contact with child protection services or avoidance of stigma. Women may have negative histories with institutions such as residential school, health care facilities, the criminal justice system or social services. They may fear that shelters will replicate past traumas. For such women, shelters are either not an option or a last resort.

Shelters can — true or not — carry the stigma of being unsafe, judgmental and rules-based. Some women find it challenging to understand how they can manage their own lives in shelters if they perceive they are relinquishing their autonomy.

It is possible to imagine a future effective shelter system. To increase the relevance, effectiveness and accessibility of shelters, we need to throw the doors open wide. We must welcome women to shelters as early in their crises as possible, mitigating the long-term negative impacts of housing instability, trauma and discrimination.

The shelter system also needs to have enough capacity to offer service on demand and reduce turn-aways. This is especially true of women-only shelters. Due to demand for space, shelters often operate at or beyond 100 per cent capacity. By reducing demand on the shelter system through effective interventions, shelters would be able to operate with a moderate vacancy rate, ensuring women have access when needed. Shelters can reduce barriers through rule reduction. When each woman's strengths are recognized and supported through self-directed case planning, women will continue to feel in charge of their lives.

The Bloom Group

In Vancouver, the Bloom Group has a fifty-year history of responding to women and women with children in crisis. On a yearly basis, we serve over 200 women and children at two shelters with eighty-four emergency beds and ten supported housing units. Over the years, countless women and families have moved through our shelters seeking a multitude of supports.

Inside the Bloom Group playroom: serving women and children in crisis

Currently, the common measure of a shelter's success is the ability to move residents quickly into housing. Historically, women and families were limited to a thirty-day shelter stay. Despite these rather severe time restrictions, some women were nonetheless lucky and able enough to move on to housing when their shelter stay expired.

In the past, housing was more available than today. Despite securing stable housing, however, and after short periods of stability, many returned to the shelter. Having moved quickly into housing without having the opportunity to more fully address underlying crises, they were challenged to maintain stability and security. There was little opportunity, given length-of-stay limitations, to address underlying issues of their homelessness. In the Bloom Group Shelters, we do not impose a predetermined length of stay; this is based on an individual case plan. The goal is always to move women on to housing as quickly as possible; however, the move is not made until other self-identified goals of recovery and strengthening have been met and the woman feels supported and ready to move.

Affordable housing stock is often unsafe, and landlords have been known to exploit women's vulnerability. Women have been sexually assaulted or forced to trade sex for a place to stay. Ill-maintained and substandard housing increases the degree of vulnerability women and families face: lack of heat or hot water, pest infestations and inadequate or no security are not uncommon. These poor living conditions often lead women to return to the shelter. The experience of leaving the shelter unprepared has often done more harm than good, creating an increased level of trauma.

In an effort to end their homelessness when their welcome has run out at the shelter, women frequently move back to the dangerous situations they had previously left. This often results in greater vulnerability, hopelessness and a diminished sense of self-worth and safety. If unable to secure housing in that short time frame, many women move to another shelter. Some women spend years bouncing from shelter to shelter without finding housing and with no time to address underlying issues; this situation compromises their stability, health and quality of life. They live in a state of permanent crisis.

As availability and affordability of rental stock have both declined in Vancouver, the demand for temporary shelter space has increased. The Bloom Group's women's and family shelters consistently run at over 100 per cent occupancy. Lengths of stays are on the rise, as are turn-aways, due to lack of shelter space. As demand for shelter space has increased, so has the complexity of issues women and families face.

Women arrive at shelters traumatized by a variety of experiences, including violence, domestic abuse, exploitation and poverty. They may be alienated from family and community.

Lack of stable housing may have resulted in job loss or interruption of education. These pressures may in turn have led to challenges with mental health and substance use, and they uniformly have resulted in an incredible amount of pain and suffering to women and families. This reality places significant pressures on the shelter system and the individuals who are working to meet the needs of women and families seeking shelter.

The future of shelters

Shelters are working to address crises, but there is potential to do so much more. There are many needs not yet being fully addressed and more possibilities to assist women and families seeking support to thrive and to be empowered to live lives with increased self-identified success and stability.

The most important first step to increase positive impact and outcomes is to improve shelter accessibility. The sooner the response to a crisis, the more the negative impacts can be mitigated. Every turn-away is a lost opportunity. An effective response to crisis will increase women's opportunities to access education, employment, income, housing and health services.

Imagine a shelter system that reduces the secondary impacts of homelessness through quick access to supports. Rebounding from crisis will be so much more effective if opportunities like education and employment can be maintained. Every turn-away risks further harm by forcing women and women with their children into unsafe situations. Delay in service increases harm to the potential service recipient just as it negatively impacts shelter staff's work environment and feeling of success. More success in providing meaningful services means more motivated and energized staff, who feel effective in their efforts to support women and children. This, in turn, reduces the risk of burnout and disinvestment in their work. The sooner a crisis is responded to, the sooner the healing can begin.

Diversion

Shelter effectiveness will be increased by greater accessibility through reduced demand. Shelters in the future will work first to prevent women from needing shelter space through effective shelter diversion practices. Outreach teams will meet women and women with children in the community *before* they become homeless. It may only take a short-term rent subsidy or debt repayment to landlords to maintain already secured housing. Supports to resolve conflicts with room-mates or landlords may help to prevent loss of housing. In some cases, a woman may be struggling to meet basic needs like buying groceries or managing the demands of maintaining her household. Assistance from a support worker could help to address this in the short term and provide support to help a woman continue to build on her capacity to manage her life independently. To prevent a woman experiencing challenges with her mental wellness from becoming homeless, a preven-tion worker could help her to identify supports and care in the community. Basing diversion teams in shelters will facilitate quick access to the shelter should diversion measures fail.

The Bloom Group addresses a woman's crisis and the resulting homelessness through safe and secure housing.

Team efforts will also benefit shelter residents in their housing searches. Shelter-based staff will build relationships with market and not-for-profit landlords to increase quick access to housing stock.

Financial supports will be available through homelessness prevention teams. Supports would include access to crisis grants for property upgrades and repairs if quality of current housing is the challenge. Crisis grants would also be used to pay outstanding rents to avoid eviction. Rent subsidies could be utilized by diversion teams in the face of financial crisis brought on by change in family makeup or job loss. Support teams will use multiple devices to prevent shelter stays. At the same time shelters will be advocates for the development of appropriate housing options. They are perfectly positioned for this work due to the service-based knowledge of individuals experiencing homelessness.

Reducing demand on shelters

Demand on shelter spaces will also be reduced by effective transition supports implemented by shelter staff as women move into housing. Staff will be well positioned for this role based on the effective and trusting relationships they have built during shelter stays. Many women in shelters express fear of moving out. Often this is related to past trauma. Sometimes it is related to challenges with mental health and/ or addictions. Women fear being re-victimized once out in the community.

Ruth was a young woman who had spent many of her childhood years in and out of shelters. Her mom, stolen from her community at a young age, struggled with the impact of growing up in a residential school. While there was much love between mother and daughter, her mom had been robbed of the opportunity to be parented by her own family. She struggled to develop the skills to keep her family together. As a teenager, Ruth became estranged from her mother and was forced into the sex trade. Having been assaulted many times in the single-room hotels she called home, Ruth returned to the shelter for safety. Ruth had every reason to believe that she would not be safe when she moved out; her past experiences had proven that to her. She would often sleep on the couch in the common area where staff could see her because she had become too afraid to sleep alone in her room. For Ruth, the path to housing was not as simple as finding a space. Ruth needed time and support to heal from her trauma and help to build on the incredible strength she had already demonstrated in surviving so much. To move from sleeping on the couch where she felt the support of twenty-four-hour staffing to closing the door on her own apartment took time. Ruth developed her own plan to slowly transition out, spending increasing lengths of time in her apartment while steadily decreasing the amount of time she slept at the shelter.

Women also fear the vulnerability created by social isolation. Transition plans must include options for gradual moves, with the possibility of residing partially in shelter and partially in housing. These strategies will help women build confidence, gain comfort and security and establish important community connections to avoid the social isolation that can so often result from the loss of housing.

Shelters will no longer operate as default long-term housing. Shelters of the future will continue to be rooted in key beliefs: that everyone deserves a place to call home; that everyone is capable of being housed and deserves the necessary time to heal in shelter and feel supported in transition. Sometimes establishing and maintaining housing may require supports beyond affordability, and shelters will play a key role in determining those supports, securing them and providing ongoing follow up. If crisis strikes after rehousing, outreach staff from shelters will move quickly to support women. Supports will include conflict resolution with landlords or roommates and establishing or re-establishing health interventions when needed. Sometimes short-term shelter respite may be the key to ensuring housing stability is continued.

Families

When families come into shelter, we see that children's ability to access education consistently and successfully has been negatively impacted by crisis. All the elements of success in school, sense of security at home, nutrition and the confidence to participate in positive social networks have been eroded by crisis. In the future, women with children will be sheltered in environments that support their family dynamic. Women will receive parenting resources to strengthen them and their bonds with their children.

It is challenging for children to thrive and moms to parent throughout crisis. The shelter environment will provide child-friendly, age-appropriate space and activities. Children and youth will be supported to maintain school attendance and community activities. Schooling is key to future success, and positive community engagement creates a safety net for children as they develop. Shelters will work with moms to ensure these supports are made possible.

One school of thought suggests that shelters should not be too comfortable, should not provide too many resources that may attract people to them as opposed to moving them toward more independent living. I disagree. I believe that shelters should offer every support possible to ensure healing, strengthening and confident self-determination. The physical environment should be spacious, comfortable and calming.

Generous spaces, where people can move about easily, help reduce conflict. Unlike the cramped quarters we live with today (in part due to overcrowding), shelters in the future will have space where women can achieve a modicum of privacy. The shelter will also have enough square footage to offer women some choice in terms of various social spaces within the facility. The more women can have choice about how and with whom to congregate, the more likely they will be able to reduce day-to-day stressors and meet their own needs.

Shelters will offer a variety of resource spaces to meet service delivery needs. Access to computers and rooms for training will provide options for capacity-building. Healing spaces for quiet reflection or therapeutic interventions will increase well-being. Culturally sensitive spaces for individuals' personal spiritual practice will provide opportunity for self-care. The high quality of the space will reduce stress and conflict, allowing for increased healing and more positive outcomes.

Women often express a need to be in the security of a safe community to heal. Shelters will support this by offering a variety of skill-building opportunities, healing and health services and peer counseling.

Indigenous women

Our shelters will acknowledge the multi-generational impact that colonization, loss of home, violence and alienation from culture and community have all had on Indigenous people. In the future, all shelters will be able to support Indigenous women overcome these impacts and fully participate in community, social and learning opportunities. Women will be supported to heal and to restore their families.

In the spirit of reconciliation, we will accept responsibility for addressing the impacts of colonization and responsibility for providing sensitive and healing supports. We will provide safe space for women and their children to securely face the challenges of overcoming the impact of colonization.

Our shelter will be culturally sensitive; supports will address the multi-generational impacts of disruption of family ties, economic inequality and inadequate health services. Shelters of the future will include Indigenous staff as a key part of service provision so that Indigenous women see themselves reflected in the staff team. Having Indigenous staff members will reduce barriers for Indigenous women seeking shelter, promote trust and relationship-building and increase feelings of hope for healing. The shelter will provide opportunities to engage in cultural practices disrupted by colonization. A path to connect to one's own culture will facilitate each woman's healing and strengthening.

Addressing crisis

Shelters of the future will catch women and their children in a caring and responsive safety net that doesn't trap them but helps them to bounce back quickly and confidently. Shelters and their staff will be adept at responding to a wide range of needs and crises. Shelters of the future will be accessible on demand. They will serve as an important safety net that provides effective care and support.

Over the years, shelter provision has advanced greatly due to increased understanding of the impact of crisis and the unique needs of women and their children. Many of the building blocks for an effective and responsive shelter system in the future are already in place.

To fully achieve the vision of shelters designed to respond effectively to crisis, however, relationships with funders will need to shift. Funders will recognize that shelters offer more than a response to homelessness. Shelter success will be measured not just through the number of housing placements but on the ability to mitigate the impact of crisis and support healing. Investment in shelter design that allows for a quality of space beyond the demand for the maximum number of beds will support the need for privacy, foster supportive and healing spaces and include space for programming.

Future shelters will increase staffing models to incorporate a variety of expertise, including flexible outreach teams. Respite and gradual transitions plans will become an accepted and funded practice. Funders will continue to support a flexible length of stay based on individual case management plans. Strong partnerships with Indigenous communities will be developed, ensuring continued advancement of healing and reparation for the impacts of colonization. Shelter providers represent an important element in responding to crisis and contributing to building healthy community. Shelter residents will be recognized as community members, not simply individuals waiting to be housed. This will require better integration with community and a greater sharing between shelter and community-based resources of expertise, training and support.

As a provider, I find it difficult to discuss the future of shelters without sounding uninterested in the solutions to homelessness. Some of my comments can leave the impression of wanting to perpetuate one's own industry. However, I believe that shelters make up a necessary part of the social safety net, one that is somewhat independent of the much larger, more complex and thornier problems of homelessness. Even if the related economic problems could somehow be solved today, the need for safe, supporting and healing places for women and women with children in crisis would still exist. I believe that treating the crises these families experience in a truly therapeutic shelter context cannot help but positively impact homelessness.

Crisis is an unfortunate part of the human condition, and women and women with children are particularly vulnerable to crisis. People will continue to face adversity, and shelters of the future need to be prepared to offer effective and timely responses. Shelters like those managed by The Bloom Group represent less a solution to homelessness than a response to crisis. By helping women and children address their crises, they have a greater chance at achieving their potential. We will have a healthier community, benefiting from the participation of all women, honouring their unique gifts and talents and helping their children to achieve their full potential. No one need be burdened by the hopelessness of unaddressed crisis.

CONCLUSION
The Way Forward for Homeless Shelters in Canada
James Hughes

Diversity

As Editor of this collection, it is clear to me that there isn't one single way forward for homeless shelters — there are many. The authors of this collection have shone their flashlights on the multiple ways shelters are organizing for the future.

- Sam Tsemberis makes the persuasive case for a shelter model that includes Housing First and the powerful impact the approach had in contributing to the massive reduction in chronic homelessness in Finland.
- Matthew Pearce, Dion Oxford, Karen Hoeft and John Rook have articulated various pathways large shelters are following to reduce

homelessness in their cities. Interestingly, they all speak about the profound importance of outreach to the communities they serve and how deepening connections with partner agencies in those communities is a prerequisite for success.

- Heather Davis, Arlene Haché and Trudi Shymka speak with one voice about the need to have specialized approaches for women facing homelessness and crisis. Violence is too often a cause of both and multiplies other challenges women face including trauma, mental illness and addiction.

- Michel Simard, Cora Gajari and Brian Duplessis describe alternative approaches smaller shelters in smaller communities might take to help homeless people make their way permanently out of shelters and off the street. Michel's model of the shelter as the social emergency room with triage and referral capacity contrasts starkly with Brian's view that shelters must advocate for the kinds of policy changes that create affordable housing and give homeless people the means and wherewithal to access it. Cora speaks eloquently about a third way, the Community Hub, that gathers into the shelter the kind of resources and skill sets to arm homeless people to permanently exit homelessness.

- The *Beyond Shelters* team from Winnipeg — Tammy Christensen, Denisa Gavan-Koop and Kelly Holmes — bring attention to the youth sector and the importance of acting quickly to prevent young people from finding themselves living a seemingly normalized life on the street. Intervening early through targeted programming adapted to youth realities offers a template for success from a Winnipeg perspective.

- The transversal theme of Indigeneity that crosses shelters large, small, women-centric and youth-centric also emerges from many of the chapters. The lessons from Winnipeg, Yellowknife, Vancouver and Regina, in particular, are that shelters must develop into organizations that are Indigenous in their very DNA in order to credibly and successfully take measures to accompany homeless Indigenous people on their journeys to a better place . . . or prevent that journey from ever being required. We learn that shelters must start by focusing inwards to examine their values, governance and programs and adapt them, with help from Elders and experts, to the cultural needs of the people they serve.

Readers may be left with the feeling that shelters are trying to be all things to all people, and they wouldn't be wrong drawing such a conclusion from this collection. Subject to a few provisos, I would suggest this is actually as it should be. Canada needs to have and should be proud to have a shelter system that is marked by difference and distinction, and even replication, for several reasons.

The first and most obvious is that the massive variety in the ages, conditions, cultures and needs of homeless people requires an equal variety in approaches, services and programs by the shelters to successfully meet the challenge. We need youth shelters, family shelters, violence-against-women-shelters and multi-service shelters to meet the needs of homeless people where and how they are. Diversity is also a form of insurance. If one shelter's methods do not suit a homeless person or entry is refused, another shelter in the city (where there is one or more) may be more suitable and accommodating. In this way, the individual is (hopefully) not left with nowhere to turn but the street (or other undesirable places).

The second reason is geography. Sheltering in the North looks a lot different than in the rest of the country in part because of its climate. Sheltering in big cities looks a lot different than in rural and remote parts of Canada because of the volume of people needing care and assistance and the resources available. Housing markets vary from Vancouver (BC) to Corner Brook (Newfoundland), and shelters need to adapt to these differences or they will fail the people they serve.

A third reason to preserve and promote heterogeneity in the community of shelters is recognition of the different skill sets that shelter leaders bring. Some leaders are better at advocacy than others, while some are better at community planning. Others still excel at interfacing with public sector institutions like hospitals and mental health agencies. The sector needs all these skills to come to bear to make a serious dent in the number of homeless in Canada.

This leads me to the last reason. To a very large extent, shelters operate as independent non-profit organizations with mandates that reflect the will of their governing boards of directors.[1] They must necessarily conduct themselves in a manner dictated by this decision-making structure. No level of government will intervene to make decisions for the shelters in terms of the clients they propose to serve or the manner they intend to serve them. Shelters can decide whether to adapt their services to a funding envelope made available by government, philanthropy or the corporate sector; they can equally decide not to bid on or contract with a particular funder. All this to say, the very nature of shelters involves being different from one other. And difference ultimately serves homeless people well . . . with a few provisos.

Provisos

The first and most important proviso is that all shelters must work on reducing and eliminating homelessness in their community. This may seem a startlingly simple caveat, but we must keep in mind that historically shelters have had other priorities that have served different purposes. The Missions during the Social Gospel period were as much about conversion to Christianity as providing desperate people with shelter and a meal. Later, many shelters were satisfied with simply providing emergency services without making any effort to use their resources to address the source of the emergency. As the pages of *Beyond Shelters* have demonstrated, modern sheltering has awoken from the reverie that a purely charitable approach to the challenge of homelessness was not only insufficient to the task but actually had the perverse effect of acclimatizing shelter clients to and entrenching them in a homeless lifestyle — the proverbial Hotel California where people "could check out but never leave." As all authors in *Beyond Shelters* have said in one way or another, shelters must know their clients by name, by history and by aspiration if they wish to successfully help them on their journey out of homelessness. This truth amounts to the prime directive of modern homeless sheltering.

The second proviso is that, while adapting services to

local conditions and specific client needs, it is incumbent on the shelters to base their service decisions on evidence. For example, well over half the authors of *Beyond Shelters* have worked to adapt their shelter's programming to include the Housing First model fully described by Sam Tsemberis in Chapter 1. While it is not the only evidence-based program focused on successfully and sustainably housing homeless people, it is probably the most studied and analyzed. As such, shelters that don't already have Housing First staff should be considering its adoption as an addition or alternative to current programming. While other programs can and should be offered in conjunction with Housing First, I think there is probably a strong argument for the network of shelters across Canada serving as the anchor for the full deployment of the Housing First vision and methodology. Reducing and eliminating at least the most chronic form of homelessness requires shelters to think and act in these terms.

Let me suggest a third and final proviso to the suggestion that diversity among shelters represents an asset for the sector and the people it serves. Homeless people, like all people, are free to choose and select the service provider they wish. With the rise in the number of homeless people over the last few decades and the consequent bulking up of the sector to serve them, we see from *Beyond Shelters* chapters that many homeless people use multiple agencies to meet their immediate needs, either sequentially or concurrently. Thus, we very often see a diverse sector serving the same person in different ways and habitually not knowing what the other agency or agencies are doing in support of their common client. Clients are often ill-served because they must tell and re-tell their stories to every organization in the circle. Rarely does one agency have the lead or the responsibility to track and share information and ensure that people's stay in the shelter system is as brief as possible. Where necessary, meaning usually in large urban centres, shelter autonomy and diversity must be adapted to work with other shelters and homeless-serving agencies in an integrated way. Client data, service options and case planning between and among shelters must be improved if we are to realize a significant reduction in homelessness in Canada.

In other words, shelter diversity constitutes a positive characteristic of our system only up to a point. If our country is going to succeed, as Finland has done, in radically reducing homelessness especially of the chronic variety, shelters will need to do their share by focusing on reducing and not managing homelessness within their facilities, deploying Housing First and other evidence-based homelessness reduction methods and working together to bring about permanent ends to homelessness for their clients.

Government

Shelters cannot and should not be expected to do this alone. Another theme that runs like a golden thread through this anthology is the role of government in the anti-homelessness movement — both directly in support of shelters and from a public policy perspective. Let's take these one at a time.

Government funding of shelters since the introduction of the original federal homelessness program in the early 2000s has been steady but unremarkable. Federal funding has helped shelters grow to meet a growing demand for their emergency services, but it has not grown in a manner to help them fully modernize and professionalize their methods, staffs and services. The shelters themselves have largely been alone in figuring out how to use evidence, how to case manage based on Housing First and how to join up their services with other shelters.[2]

However, as Sam Tsemberis discussed in his chapter, the federal government profoundly shifted how federal homelessness funding was used in 2014 when it required communities to allocate at least 50 per cent of available funding to Housing First programming (though unfortunately this positive shift did not come with any increase in actual funding). The most recent iteration of the federal strategy in 2018 actually targets reducing the number of chronically homeless people by 50 per cent overall across the country by, in part, providing municipalities with more flexibility in how they use federal homelessness spending. The new rules only come into effect in 2019, so we'll all have to wait and see their impact.[3]

Provincial and municipal funding have in some places been creative and generous on the housing front, making capital dollars available to shelters to build, buy and renovate facilities for homeless people. An overall reduction in the number of shelter clients between 2005 and 2014 (by almost 20,000 people) is testimony to intelligent investments and partnerships in this respect. However, the rise in the average length of shelter stays indicates that a great deal more housing investment is needed. As the authors of this anthology have articulated so often and so well, addressing the housing needs of a more complex and harder-to-house population of homeless people, those whom we have classified as the "chronically homeless," requires even more investment in exit services and supportive permanent housing than ever before.

Another area both levels of government need to examine is payment for success models that are being experimented with in other jurisdictions.[4] Shelter funding models that finance on a *per diem* or *per capita* basis are not aligned with the vision of reducing and eliminating homelessness. Most shelters are still funded in this way, meaning the more clients they have and the bigger they are, the more money they'll receive. There are certainly other funding models in use (including simple annual cost of living increases), but governments, as key funders, can encourage shelters to move toward reducing emergency services while growing their capacity to provide homelessness-ending programs like Housing First, homecare support and actually owning and managing housing units for formerly homeless people.

In addition to more creative and significant housing investments and funding envelopes that align with homelessness reduction values, both federal and provincial governments must consider other policy levers they can deploy to be more targeted and successful in their own efforts to reduce and eliminate homelessness in Canada. Let me suggest two, both inspired from initiatives in the United Kingdom.

The first is the creation of a What Works Centre on Homelessness.[5] What Works Centres are independent research organizations that advise both policy-makers and practitioners about the state of the evidence in a given field. There are ten What Works Centres in the U.K. focusing on such policy topics as local economic development, child welfare, education, crime reduction and ageing. A new What Works Centre is emerging for the homelessness sector called the Centre for Homelessness Impact.[6] It will be a very useful source of guidance for the sector, including shelters, to access the best methods on reducing homelessness for a wide variety of clienteles in a language that is understandable and clear (as opposed to the too often cryptic academic summaries that are currently available).

Anther promising development is the adoption by the

U.K. Parliament of the *Homelessness Reduction Act* (2017).[7] The legislation requires local housing authorities to take steps to refer homeless people in their communities to specialized resources, including housing opportunities. The legislation has quite rightly been criticized for failing to offer the necessary resources to local housing authorities to put such a referral system fully into place or to address the root causes of homelessness, but the seeds of a promising legislative initiative have nonetheless been sown.[8] A Canadian version of this legislation should entrench a right to housing. It should also require funded agencies, including shelters, to collect and share client data (in a manner that respects privacy rights) and participate in community planning efforts to reduce homelessness.

Prevention

Many authors in this collection have discussed the need to reduce homelessness by preventing it in the first place. Several are either actively in the prevention space already (Ndinawe in Winnipeg) or are soon to be active in that sphere (Old Brewery Mission in Montreal). I predict more aggressive activity on the prevention front going forward. For example, Raising the Roof, a national organization whose mission is to prevent homelessness, is prototyping The Upstream Project to assess high school students for risk of homelessness and rapidly intervene to prevent loss of housing when the risk level reaches code red.[9] There's no reason this and other like projects can't be scaled through the shelter network.

Beyond shelters

My time at the Old Brewery Mission was very special to me. The learning curve was incredibly steep, but my teachers — the shelter staff and clients — were mercifully patient as

I and our Board of Directors struggled to figure out how to stop being a merry-go-round for homeless people; we expected them to wait every day and night for their meal, shower and bed without hope or expectation that they could or would ever be able to leave such a way of life.

I remember vividly a presentation I made near the end of my tenure. I was describing how the Mission had adopted a homelessness reduction mantra, begun to staff up (with the collaboration of the union that represented employees) to help accompany "our" people permanently out of homelessness, transformed our facilities and built and managed permanent housing for formerly destitute people (like "Clifford" described so caringly by Sam Tsemberis). I wondered out loud at the end of my presentation whether our organization was still a "shelter" or whether it had become something else — like a social services agency for homeless people or a housing service.

In the end, whatever we might have called it (and, as Matthew Pearce explains, the Mission is now leagues ahead of where it was back in 2008 when I left), the organization was truly "beyond shelter" and, like hundreds of other similar organizations across Canada, was never turning back.

Contributor Bios

Tammy Christensen is the Executive Director of Ndinawemaaganag Endaawaad Inc., a youth-serving organization that provides a holistic continuum of services to improve social, economic, cultural and personal outcomes for Indigenous youth in Winnipeg. Previously Tammy worked with the Ma Mawi Wi Chi Itata where she served in a variety of roles supporting Indigenous children, youth, and families. Tammy is also the co-chair of Here and Now: Winnipeg's Plan to End Youth Homelessness Governance Steering Committee.

Heather Davis is the Executive Director at Willow House in Corner Brook, Newfoundland. Her career path has meandered through many aspects of community development, but her focus as a proud feminist has always been on working to establish and grow healthy, vibrant communities that are safe for every person, regardless of sex, status or circumstance. She has a Master's degree in Sociology from the University of Guelph and lives in her hometown with her partner Chris and their three beautiful sons, Gabe, Hudson and Finn.

Brian Duplessis was most recently the Executive Director of the United Way of Central New Brunswick. Prior to that, he was the Executive Director of the Fredericton Homeless Shelters. In just under three years at the shelters, Brian led significant change. By bringing community groups and government agencies together, long-term clients were successfully transitioned back into the community and a dangerous environment was transformed into a much safer one. Overall use of the shelters declined significantly. Brian grew up in a challenging environment in public housing in Saint John, New Brunswick, but went on to a successful international career in corporate communications and government relations. After returning to Canada to take up an executive position with NB Power, he moved into the non-profit world including serving a term as co-Chair of the Board of Directors for the Economic and Social Inclusion

Corporation, the Crown Corporation established to implement the province's Poverty Reduction Plan. In 2009, the University of New Brunswick's Renaissance College presented him with their Unsung Leader's Award for the work he has done on poverty issues in the community.

Cora Gajari has been working in community in the area of poverty and homelessness in Regina for approximately ten years. Prior to that she worked for the provincial government as a policy analyst in the areas of justice and Aboriginal employment development. She has a BA Honours and Master's of Arts degree in Sociology with a focus on the application of social theories to racism, Indigenous peoples and social systems. She is the mother of seven and grandmother of six, and is a member of the Inuvialuit of the Inuvik region.

Denisa Gavan-Koop is the Coordinator of Here and Now: Winnipeg's Plan to End Youth Homelessness. Denisa has dedicated her career to community development and public engagement in the non-profit and private sectors. Driven by her focus to collaboratively build inclusive, equitable and resilient communities, she has designed, coordinated and led engagement initiatives and planning processes for community master plans, campus plans and strategic plans. She is dedicated to developing strategies that support inclusive and healthy communities through meaningful engagement opportunities.

Arlene Haché is a grassroots woman who has experienced homelessness and traumatic impacts of childhood and youth violence. She is well known across Canada's Arctic as an advocate for social change and as a result of her work was awarded the Order of Canada in 2009 and then the Queen Elizabeth II Diamond Jubilee Medal in 2012. Arlene is a published author and has participated on several research teams that give voice to people with lived experience. She currently works as a Program Developer with the Temiskaming Native Women's Support Group and provides technical support to the District of Temiskaming Elders Council. She serves as a Director on several national Canadian boards addressing issues related to mental health and homelessness and currently sits on the Governing Council of the Huairou Commission. Arlene also sat on the national Advisory Committee on Homelessness chaired by the Honourable Adam Vaughan.

Karen Hoeft has been a Salvation Army Officer for over thirty years. She has been an advocate to bring together many different sectors to build community-based capacity to respond to the need for affordable and adequate housing for all Canadians. She has been actively involved in running emergency shelters for over twenty years. She chaired the Coalition to end Homelessness in Yellowknife; partnered with the At Home/Chez Soi Study for the Winnipeg location; was a Citizen Board Member for the Winnipeg Housing Rehabilitation Corporation; and participated on the Steering Committee for the establishing of the Bell Hotel Housing First Project in Winnipeg. She believes that when we work together real change is possible and we can build a better world.

Kelly Holmes is the Executive Director of Resource Assistance for Youth (RaY), a non-profit street level agency working with street-entrenched and homeless youth up to the age of twenty-nine. RaY is non-judgmental and non-partisan, employing a harm reduction approach to all interactions with youth in need. RaY offers a variety of support and resources to youth including intermediate needs such as street outreach, meals and advocacy, housing supports, health and wellness, and employment and education. Kelly is also the co-chair of Here and Now: Winnipeg's Plan to End Youth Homelessness Governance Steering Committee.

Dion Oxford was the Mission Strategist for the Salvation Army's five homeless shelters in Toronto, called Housing and Homeless Supports. Dion, along with his wife Erinn and daughter Cate, live in Toronto and are committed to journeying alongside people at the margins of society. He has spent more than twenty-five years working among folks who are living on or close to the streets of Toronto. He was the founding director of the Salvation Army Gateway, a shelter for men experiencing homelessness.

Matthew Pearce has been the President and Chief Executive Officer of the Old Brewery Mission since 2008. Through media and public events, he shares the Mission's vision to see the end of homelessness in our lifetime, engaging the public about practical and sustainable solutions to help homeless men and women reclaim their lives. He sits on the Board of Directors of the Centre Hospitalier de l'Université de Montréal as well as the Canadian Alliance to End Homelessness, the Montreal Movement to End Homelessness and the Communauté Saint-Urbain. A graduate in History and Political Science from Dalhousie University in Nova Scotia, he has devoted most of his career to not-for-profit causes, including twenty-two years in the field of international development through his service with Canada World Youth, which he was the President and CEO of from 1999 to 2005.

Dr. John Rook is a passionate servant leader who champions the belief that poverty can be solved. With a doctorate from Oxford University, he has spent years both at the front lines and in academia to gain both a theoretical and practical understanding of the issues facing people in poverty. For six years he chaired the National Council of Welfare. From 2000 to 2010, he worked for the Salvation Army and for six years was CEO of their Community Services which included the Booth Centre and Centre of Hope homeless projects. He has received numerous recognitions for his work including the Queen Elizabeth II Diamond Jubilee Medal (2013). As a member of the Alberta Provincial Interagency Council on Homelessness he chaired the Research Committee. He is the Founding Director of the Canadian Poverty Institute at Ambrose University in Calgary and currently is Director of Strategic Initiatives and Managing Director (Calgary) for the Mustard Seed Society.

Trudi Shymka is the Associate Executive Director for The Bloom Group in Vancouver, BC, and has supported the growth and development of its shelter and affordable housing programs for twenty-five years. Under her guidance, these programs have become recognized specialists in providing low-barrier care for marginalized and Indigenous women. Trudi has also served in leadership positions on the boards of Greater Vancouver Shelter Strategy, Shelter Net BC, and the Homelessness Services Association of BC.

Michel Simard began a journey of self-discovery after being homeless for several years in the seventies. He travelled the world, studied criminology and theology at the University of Montreal and, in 1989, began working with homeless people in Trois-Rivières. He became the Executive Director of the Centre Le Havre in 1993 and transformed the shelter into a model for integrated social emergency practice in Canada. He retired from Le Havre in 2016 but continues to dedicate his life to the power of compassionate living to drive social transformation.

Dr. Sam Tsemberis is a clinical-community psychologist who developed the Housing First model. He serves as President/CEO of the Pathways Housing First Institute and faculty Department of Psychiatry, of New York Presbyterian Hospital, Columbia University Medical Center. He is also Clinical Director for Housing First for Youth, Canada. His Housing First program is now implemented across the United States, Canada, the EU, and New Zealand and is an integral approach in national policies on homelessness. Dr. Tsemberis has published many articles and book chapters. He has received numerous honours and awards including the American Psychiatric Association's Gold Award for Community Mental Health Programs and the Distinguished Contribution to Independent Practice Award from the American Psychological Association.

Endnotes and References

Introduction

Notes

1. See James Hughes, *Early Intervention* (Toronto: James Lorimer & Co., 2015), p. 148.

2. Alan Hustak, *Soup to Self Sufficiency: Montreal's Old Brewery Mission* (Montreal: Old Brewery Mission, 2014), p. 36.

3. See Salvation Army Canada website at: https://www.salvationarmy. ca/what-we-do/in-your-community/housing-and-shelters/.

4. See Salvation Army website at: https://www.salvationarmy.ca/ about-us/missionandvalues/.

5. Jean Dupuis, *Homelessness: The U.S. and Canadian Experience* (September 12, 2000), retrieved from http://publications.gc.ca/ Collection-R/LoPBdP/BP/prb0002-e.htm.

6. Stephen Gaetz, Erin Dej, Tim Richter and Melanie Redman, *The State of Homelessness in Canada 2016* (Toronto: Canadian Observatory on Homelessness Press, 2016), retrieved from http://homelesshub. ca/sites/default/files/SOHC16_final_20Oct2016.pdf.

7. Employment and Social Development Canada, *Shelter Capacity Report 2016*, retrieved from https://www.canada.ca/en/employment-social-development/programs/communities/homelessness/ publications-bulletins/shelter-capacity-2016.html.

8. Ibid.

9. Gaetz, Dej, Richter and Redman, *State of Homelessness in Canada*, p. 30.

10. Ibid, p. 31.

11. National Alliance to End Homelessness, *Housing First* (April 20, 2016), retrieved from https://endhomelessness.org/resource/housing-first/.

Chapter 1

References

Anthony, W. A. (2000). A recovery-oriented service system: Setting some system level standards. *Psychiatric Rehabilitation Journal*, 24(2), 159–169.

Aubry, T., Farrell, S., Hwang, S. W., & Calhoun, M. (2013). Identifying the patterns of emergency shelter stays of single individuals in Canadian cities of different sizes. *Housing Studies*, 28(6), 910–927.

Aubry, T., Tsemberis, S., Adair, C. E., Veldhuizen, S., Streiner, D., Latimer, E., . . . & Goering, P. (2015). One year outcomes of a randomized controlled trial of Housing First in five Canadian cities. *Psychiatric Services, 66*(5), 463–469.

Damschroder, L. J., Aron, D. C., Keith, R. E., Kirsh, S. R., Alexander, J. A., & Lowery, J. C. (2009). Implementation of health services research findings into practice: A consolidated framework for advancing implementation science. *Implementation Science, 4*(1), 50–59.

Deal, C., Lessin, T., & Moore, M. (Producers), & Moore, M. (Director). (2015). *Where to invade next* [Motion picture]. United States: Dog Eat Dog Films & IMG Films.

Employment and Social Development Canada. (2014). *Homelessness Partnering Strategy*. Retrieved from https://www.canada.ca/en/employment-social-development/programs/communities/homelessness.html.

Felton, B. J. (2003). Innovation and implementation in mental health services for homeless adults: A case study. *Community Mental Health Journal, 39*(4), 309–322.

Flynn, N. (2004). *Another bullshit night in suck city*. New York, NY: W. W. Norton.

O'Sullivan, E. (2017, November 7). *Homelessness in Ireland and Norway (Finland and Denmark)*. Presentation to the Focus Ireland / Trinity College School of Social Work and Social Policy Seminar, Royal Irish Academy, Dublin, Ireland.

Padgett, D., Henwood, B. F., & Tsemberis, S. J. (2016). *Housing First: Ending homelessness, transforming systems, and changing lives*. New York, NY: Oxford University Press.

Poulin, S. R., Maguire, M., Metraux, S., & Culhane, D. (2011). Service use and costs for persons experiencing chronic homelessness in Philadelphia: A population-based study. *Psychiatric Services, 61*(11), 1093–1098.

Prochaska, J. O., & DiClemente, C. C. (1983). Stages and processes of self-change of smoking: Toward an integrative model of change. *Journal of Consulting and Clinical Psychology, 51*(3), 390–395.

Segaert, A. (2012). *The National Shelter Study: Emergency shelter use in Canada 2005–2009*. Retrieved from http://homelesshub.ca/sites/default/files/Homelessness Partnering Secretariat 2013 Segaert_0.pdf.

Stefancic, A., & Tsemberis, S. (2007). Housing First for long-term shelter dwellers with psychiatric disabilities in a suburban county: A four-year study of housing access and retention. *Journal of Primary Prevention, 28*, 265–279.

Stefancic, A., Tsemberis, S., Messeri, P., Drake, R., & Goering, P. (2013). The Pathways Housing First fidelity scale for programs serving individuals with psychiatric disabilities. *American Journal of Psychiatric Rehabilitation, 16*, 240–261.

Tsemberis, S. (2015). *Pathways Housing First: Ending Homelessness for Individuals with Mental Illness and Addiction.* Centre City, MN: Hazelden Publishing.

Upshaw, J. (2018, January 24). First national director of Housing First programme appointed. *Dublin Gazette.* Retrieved from https://dublingazette.com/news/first-national-director-housing-first-programme-appointed/.

Y-Foundation. (2017). *A home of your own: Housing First and ending homelessness in Finland.* Retrieved from https://ysaatio.fi/assets/files/2018/01/A_Home_of_Your_Own_lowres_spreads.pdf.

Chapter 2

Notes

1. Shelter turn-aways mean admission is not permitted. Shelter staff instead work to assist the woman in finding support elsewhere, and provide referrals and advocacy to ensure she stays safe by connecting her to other services.

2. Provincial Operational Standards were developed by the Newfoundland and Labrador Department of Health & Community Services, Regional Health Authorities, THANL and some of the Executive Directors of Transition Houses. Acknowledging that transition houses "serve as a lifeline for women experiencing abuse by providing essential safety and support services," the aim of the Operational Standards document is to "promote excellence in that work by defining the quality to which Transition Houses aspire" (2010). It contains standards on everything from confidentiality to intake procedures to file retention and destruction. At the time of writing, it has not been reviewed in eight years and requires substantial revision to be in line with current shelter philosophies and practices.

3. Shelters were housed with the Department of Health provincially before being devolved to regional health authorities in the early 2000s. The move to another department was lobbied for by THANL because of unresolved issues and discrepancies between shelters and health authorities. The decision to move to Newfoundland and Labrador Housing Corporation was taken by the Newfoundland and Labrador government.

Chapter 3

Notes

1. For five years, I wrote a biweekly column called "Poverty Matters" for the Fredericton *Daily Gleaner*. I cited the LeBlanc interviews in one of these columns.

2. "Opioid Epidemic," Poverty Matters column, Fredericton *Daily Gleaner*, March 26, 2009.

Chapter 7

Notes

1. Rossbrook House presentation to the City of Winnipeg Executive Policy Committee (December 8, 2016), retrieved from http://clkapps.winnipeg.ca/DMIS/ViewPdf.asp?SectionId=453863.

2. Indigenous Services Canada, "Minister Philpott to Announce Funding for Indigenous Youth Resource Centre in Winnipeg" (March 27, 2018), retrieved from https://www.canada.ca/en/indigenous-services-canada/news/2018/03/minister-philpott-to-announce-funding-for-indigenous-youth-resource-centre-in-winnipeg.html.

3. "Organization Hits $25K Crowdfunding Goal for Youth Safe Space in West End," *CBC News*, December 13, 2015, retrieved from http://www.cbc.ca/news/canada/manitoba/organization-hits-25k-crowdfunding-goal-for-youth-safe-space-in-west-end-1.3363456.

4. Christina Maes Nino, Maria Godoy, Scott McCullough, Brent Retzlaff, Al Wiebe and Larry Wurcherer, *The Winnipeg Street Census 2015: Final Report* (Winnipeg: Social Planning Council of Winnipeg, 2016), retrieved from https://winnipeg.ca/cms/pdfs/WSC_FinalReport.pdf.

5. J. David Hulchanski, Philippa Campsie, Shirley B. Y. Chau, Stephen W. Hwang and Emily Paradis, "Introduction: Homelessness: What's in a Word," in *Finding Home: Policy Options for Addressing Homelessness in Canada* (Toronto: University of Toronto, Cities Centre, 2009), retrieved from http://homelesshub.ca/sites/default/files/FindingHome_Full.pdf.

6. Census Data, 2016.

7. Ibid.

8. Stephen Gaetz, Tanya Gulliver and Tim Richter, *The State of Homelessness in Canada 2014* (Toronto: Homeless Hub Press, 2014), retrieved from http://homelesshub.ca/sites/default/files/SOHC2014.pdf.

9. Uri Bronfenbrenner, "Towards an Experimental Ecology of Human Development," *American Psychologist* 32, no. 7 (1977): 513–531.

10. Lewis Williams and Zubia Mumtaz, *Being Alive and Well: Aboriginal Youth and Evidence-Based Approaches to Promoting Mental Well-Being* (Saskatoon: Prairie Region Health Promotion Centre, 2007).

11. Campaign 2000, *Manitoba Child and Family Poverty Report Card, 2016*, retrieved from https://campaign2000.ca/wp-content/uploads/2016/03/MBRC2014.pdf.

12. Maes Nino, Godoy, McCullough, Retzlaff, Wiebe and Wurcherer, *Winnipeg Street Census 2015*.

13. Province of Manitoba, *Family Services Annual Reports*, 2017.

14. Ibid.

15. Maes Nino, Godoy, McCullough, Retzlaff, Wiebe and Wurcherer, *Winnipeg Street Census 2015*.

16. Paul Memmott and Catherine Chambers, "Indigenous Homelessness in Australia: An Introduction," *Parity* 23, no. 9 (2010): 10.

17. Jesse Thistle, *Indigenous Definition of Homelessness in Canada* (Toronto: Canadian Observatory on Homelessness Press, 2017), retrieved from http://homelesshub.ca/sites/default/files/COHIndigenousHomelessness-summary.pdf.

18. Aboriginal Standing Committee on Housing and Homelessness, 2012.

19. "Social Services Workers Pen Plan to Tackle Youth Homelessness," *CBC News*, October 11, 2016, retrieved from http://www.cbc.ca/news/canada/manitoba/winnipeg-youth-homeless-plan-launches-1.3800983.

Chapter 9

Notes

1. See John Rook and Samantha Sexsmith, "The Criminalization of Poverty" in John Winterdyck, ed., *Crime Prevention: International Perspectives, Issues and Trends* (Boca Raton, FL: CRC Press, 2017), pp. 317–344.

2. See the Calgary RESOLVE campaign at www.resolvecampaign.com as an excellent example of government, not-for-profit and business working together on solutions. The program raised over $70 million for affordable housing in Calgary.

3. Visit the Safe Communities Opportunity and Resource Centre online at www.scorce.ca.

4. Toronto: James Lorimer & Co., 2015.

Chapter 11

References

Bonilla-Silva, E. (2010). *Racism without racists: Color-blind racism and the persistence of racial inequality in America* (3rd ed.). Lanham, MD: Rowman & Littlefield.

Chinowsky, P. (2008). Staircase model for new practice implementation. *Journal of Management in Engineering, 24*(3), 187–195.

Christensen, J. (2012). "They want a different life": Rural northern settlement dynamics and pathways to homelessness in Yellowknife and Inuvik, Northwest Territories. *Canadian Geographer, 56*(4), 419–438.

Churchill, W. (2002). *Struggle for the land: Native North American resistance to genocide, ecocide and colonization.* San Francisco, CA: City Lights.

Doob, C. B. (2013). *Social inequality and social stratification in U.S. Society.* Upper Saddle River, NJ: Pearson.

Falvo, N. (2008, Special Edition). The "Housing First" model: Immediate access to permanent housing. *Canadian Housing, 32*–35.

Falvo, N. (2011). *Homelessness in Yellowknife: An emerging social challenge.* Toronto: The Canadian Homelessness Research Network Press.

Fasta, E., & Collin-Vézina, D. (2010). Historical trauma, race-based trauma and resilience of Indigenous Peoples: A literature review. *First Peoples Child and Family Review, 5*(1), 126–136. Retrieved from http://www.fncaringsociety.com/sites/default/files/online-journal/vol5num1/Fast-Collin-Vezina_pp126.pdf.

Four Worlds Centre for Development. (2007, November). *Learning you just blink and it can happen: A study of women's homelessness north of 60* (Pan-Territorial report). Retrieved from http://ywcacanada.ca/data/publications/00000009.pdf.

Klodawsky, F. (2009). Home spaces and rights to the city: Thinking social justice for chronically homeless women. *Urban Geography, 30*(6), 591–610. https://doi.org/10.2747/0272-3638.30.6.591.

Mitchell, T. L., & Maracle, D. T. (2005). Healing the generations: Post-traumatic stress and the health status of Aboriginal populations in Canada. *Journal of Aboriginal Health, 2,* 14–23. Retrieved from http://www.naho.ca/jah/english/jah02_01/JournalVol2No1ENG4headinggenerations.pdf.

Neal, R. (2004). *Voices: Women, poverty and homelessness in Canada.* Retrieved from http://ywcacanada.ca/data/research_docs/00000275.pdf.

Royal Commission on Aboriginal Peoples. (1996). *Looking forward, looking back* (Vol. 1). Retrieved from https://qspace.library.queensu.ca/bitstream/1974/6874/5/RRCAP1_combined.pdf.

Sakamoto, I., Ricciardi, J., Plyler, J., Wood, N., Chapra, A., Chin, M., . . . & Nunes, M. (2010). *Coming together: Homeless women, housing and social support.* Toronto: Wellesley Institute.

Schertow, J. A. (2006, December 15). Colonialism, genocide and gender violence: Indigenous women. *IC Magazine.* Retrieved from https://intercontinentalcry.org/colonialism-genocide-and-gender-violence-indigenous-women/.

Simpson, L. (2014, March 5). Not murdered and not missing [Web log message]. Retrieved from http://nationsrising.org/not-murdered-and-not-missing/.

Smith, A., & Ross, L. (2004). Introduction: Native women and state violence. *Social Justice, 31*(4), 1–7. Retrieved from https://www.socialjusticejournal.org/SJEdits/98Edit.html.

Stakeholder interviews, 2011/2012 Organizational Assessment, Yellowknife Women's Centre.

Stannard, D. (1992). *American holocaust.* Oxford, UK: Oxford University Press.

Thistle, J. (2017). *Indigenous Definition of Homelessness in Canada.* Toronto: Canadian Observatory on Homelessness Press. Retrieved from http://homelesshub.ca/sites/default/files/COHIndigenousHomelessness-summary.pdf.

Webster, A. (2006). *Homelessness in the Territorial North: State and availability of the knowledge.* Retrieved from http://www.homelesshub.ca/sites/default/files/NRP_North_Homelessness_Report_Final_30_Oct_06_0.pdf.

Conclusion

Notes

1. The City of Toronto directly manages several shelters for homeless people including one of Canada's largest, Seaton House. The facilities are not independent non-profits but public shelters managed by the municipality.

2. The new federal Homeless Individuals and Families Information System data gathering and sharing tool together with the recently announced federal initiative entitled "Coordinated Access System" may go some way toward correcting this reality. See Canadian Alliance to End Homelessness, *What Is a Coordinated Access System?*, at http://caeh.ca/cas/.

3. See Jordan Press, "Federal Government Unveils Changes to Its Strategy for Fighting Homelessness," *Toronto Star*, June 10, 2018, retrieved from https://www.thestar.com/news/canada/2018/06/10/federal-government-announces-changes-to-its-strategy-fighting-homelessness.html.

4. See for example Department for Communities and Local Government, *Qualitative Evaluation of the London Homelessness Social Impact Bond (SIB): Final Report* (November 2017), retrieved from https://assets.publishing.service.gov.uk/government/uploads/system/uploads/attachment_data/file/658921/Qualitative_Evaluation_of_the_London_Homelessness_SIB.pdf.

5. See U.K. Government, What Works Network, retrieved from https://www.gov.uk/guidance/what-works-network.

6. See Centre for Homeless Impact website at https://www.homelessnessimpact.org/.

7. The *Act* can be found at http://www.legislation.gov.uk/ukpga/2017/13/contents/enacted.

8. See Patrick Butler, "New Homelessness Act Fails to Address Root Causes, Charities Say," *The Guardian*, April 3, 2018, retrieved from https://www.theguardian.com/society/2018/apr/03/homelessness-act-england-councils-legal-duty-fails-address-root-causes-charities-say.

9. See https://www.raisingtheroof.org/what-we-do/our-initiatives/the-upstream-project/.

Index